THE STONE AND
THE GLORY
STUDY GUIDE

GREG HARRIS

KRESS
BIBLICAL
RESOURCES

The Stone and the Glory Study Guide

© 2009 Greg Harris

Published by:

P.O. Box 132228
The Woodlands, TX 77393
www.kressbiblical.com

ISBN 978-1-934952-10-8

Cover Design: Mario Kushner
Text Design: Valerie Moreno

Significant contributions made (written, verbally or both) in order of appearance: H. J. B. Chris E. Bush, Bradley A. U. Sewell, Kevin McAteer, Paula Adams, Rebecca R. Howard, John MacArthur, Jeff Terrell, Micah Chung, Gabriel Powell, Pat Rotisky, Dana Hilborn, Holly Swanson, Midori Firestone—and continuously, as still one untimely born and grafted in, Johnny McClaughlin.

Contents

The Dedication of *The Stone and the Glory*

*A*nyone who is in ministry has benefitted from the lives of godly people. For those who are blessed enough to attend a good seminary, some of the greatest blessings one has is to interact with professors. Drs. Jim Rosscup and Robert Thomas were such individuals (among others) who to this day have affected my life and ministry by their own lives.

These men are both quite different and yet similar in their love for the Lord and for His Word. I had Dr. Jim Rosscup for many classes. I was a Bible Exposition major, and he chaired the department at that time at Talbot Theological Seminary. He is a thorough scholar with a desire to honor God with his meticulous preparation for all of his classes. "Jim Rosscup Bible Notes" are some of my most prized—and used—possessions.

Yet, beyond the scholarly expertise that he brings, Jim Rosscup is a man of God and a man of prayer. So often he has humbled me by his godliness. Often I would be grumbling to myself about something, and Jim Rosscup would say something in class, send a note to me (and many other students), or just make a comment to me in passing. He would be oblivious to the fact that his godly life and responses were so different from mine, and I learned so much about God and being a man of God (in progress) from just observing him. Of the many times I have eaten with him or met with him in private, I cannot recall one time where I did not learn something. His commitment to his beloved wife Mildred, who just recently went home to be with her Lord, gave many others and me a new definition of what being a "one woman man" means. I am a much better man, husband, father, and teacher because of this dear man of God.

Dr. Robert Thomas became more of an influence after I graduated. I had him for different classes at Talbot. Somewhere along the line I started calling him "Dr. Bob." I don't even remember asking permission to do so; I think I just did it. Dr. Bob was considered a "terror in the classroom" by some, and his assignments were massive ("You are *killing* me with this assignment, Dr. Bob!" I would say out loud at my apartment as I attempted to complete the requirements for his classes). Yet, I found him to be gracious and very approachable, plus to this day he is one of the sharpest, dry wits I have ever encountered.

Dr. Bob greatly influenced me in two significant ways. First, with the Greek exegetical digests that he produced, along with his other writings. All my "Dr. Bob Books" are saturated with highlights and notes I wrote in the margins. Some of them look like they could fall apart at any time, they have been used that often. That is a tremendous compliment to any book.

Second, after I had graduated from Talbot and later Dallas Theological Seminary, Dr. Bob and I would meet each year at the Evangelical Theological Society's national convention. I would always write to him a few months early to see if he had time for a meal. We would usually meet for breakfast, have a couple of hours together, "solve the world's problems," and just talk. By this stage in my life I did not need anything from him as a reference, was very happy where I was in my ministry, and just enjoyed learning from an older man of God who also happened to be a world-class scholar. We did these yearly meetings eight or nine times. I know I got the better end of the deal. By the way, in all our yearly meetings we never once talked about my teaching at The Master's Seminary.

It is with my utmost joy and delight that all the royalties from *The Stone and the Glory* and *The Stone and the Glory Study Guide* go to The Master's Seminary (www.tms.edu). I very much am praying for "double fruit," that God uses both the book and the royalties to help the school in whatever way they see fit to use them.

One final note: all the Glory Books and study guides are or will be translated into Spanish, Arabic, Mandarin, and German (plus whatever other languages God sees fit). For those interested, you can keep track of these at www.glorybooksministry.org.

To God be the Glory!

Greg Harris
August 2009
The Master's Seminary

The Writing of **The Stone and the Glory**

*T*he Cup and the Glory* was written in October–December 1996, but was not published until ten years later. I received my first copy of the book on March 2, 2006. As explained in "The Writing of *The Cup and the Glory*" section of *The Cup and the Glory Study Guide*, I did not intend to write a book. It was only toward the end of writing it that I concluded, "Well, I guess it's a book." Up through the last two chapters, I studied and wrote for myself. God was healing me spiritually and emotionally and indeed "perfecting, confirming, strengthening, and establishing" me (1 Pet. 5:10). There was a divine compulsion and a personal delight to dig into God's Word and try to discover answers from it. Although "The Wilderness" was extremely hard and frustrating, I look back on the process of researching and writing what would become *The Cup and the Glory* as one of my sweetest times with the Lord. I was a little sad when it ended and I had no immediate plans of writing another book.

My plans, however, are not God's plans, and much to my surprise, I began another book about a year later. The first four chapters of *The Darkness and the Glory* were written in July 1997, during a very intense summer school class. You can read about this in "The Writing of *The Darkness and the Glory*" in *The Darkness and the Glory Study Guide*. The process for writing was different in that, first, I had already written a book (although it was not yet published) and second, I knew *The Darkness and the Glory* was going to be a book before I ever wrote the first word. (I had no idea if it would be published or not, but I wrote this one as a complete book instead of just individual chapters that turned into a book). Since I was teaching my first year at Southeastern Baptist Theological Seminary as well as completing the Th.D. program at Dallas Theological Seminary, I only occasionally worked on the remainder of the book, and completed it sometime around May 1998. I did not take exact notes because I had no idea anyone would be interested in this years later.

I do not want to misrepresent the process in writing *The Darkness in the Glory* to say that I haphazardly worked on it. It greatly affected me to write many of the chapters within the book. Most were done (especially the early chapters) with much weeping. Being a new professor at a new school and trying to finish a massive dissertation took much time away from the writing. However, when the time came to write, God helped me "lock in" to what I was doing. The last chapters, as one might expect, were joyous celebrations of some of the victories won by Jesus at Calvary. I hated for the writing of that book to end.

In June 2000 I taught a summer class at Jordan Evangelical Theological Seminary in Amman, Jordan. I took a student who became a God-given friend named Chris Bush with me. Chris read the rough draft of *The Darkness and the Glory* during our two-week time in Jordan. It affected him deeply, and it was delightful for me to talk with someone about what I had written. Chris was probably about the fourth or fifth person to read this. We were able to visit Machaerus (where John the Baptist was imprisoned and beheaded). It was my second time there and Chris' first. (More about that in the introduction to the chapter entitled "The One").

In September 2000 I began the sketchpad for *The Stone and the Glory*. (It would not be until March 2006 that *The Cup and the Glory* was published and then December 2008 for the publication of *The Darkness and the Glory*). The "sketchpad" is the research of the material, the thinking through the logic of the book, and the breakdown of the content and the order of the chapters. It takes a long time (but is such a delight to do). By the time I am done with the sketchpad, I know what I am going to write; then it is just a matter of how to say it. I presume this is how an artist does a portrait of someone. Of course, there would be a lot of editing and tweaking over the years, and again, I had no idea if it would ever be published.

For most years when I was teaching, I would attend the Evangelical Theological Society's national convention. It is held in different cities the week before Thanksgiving. The one in November 14-17, 2000, was at The Opryland Hotel in Nashville, Tennessee. I had a room to myself and was able to spread out the many sheets of the book on the adjacent bed and chairs in my room. I would take breaks and visit with friends I had not seen for a year or longer (such as Dr. Imad Shehadeh from Jordan or Dr. Robert Thomas from The Master's Seminary) and attend a few sessions, but for the most part, I did nothing but start in chapter one and write as much as I could during this cluster of days. I would begin around 3:00 AM and write the entire day (with a few breaks) until I knew I had hit my limit where I just could not think straight anymore. I would dine with a friend, see a few people, go to bed early and then begin the process all over again.

I wrote about eight chapters those days, but I did not have time to read them. Email had just recently become popular, so I would send the chapters as an attachment for Chris Bush to read. Although Chris hails from New Jersey, and proudly and quite frequently talks in glowing terms about his northern heritage, he had moved to Florida for a segment of his life. Technically speaking, Chris Bush was the first to read *The Stone and the Glory*, even before I did, because writing the book is a much different process than reading it, and I knew I would go back and read it in due time. Since he had read the previous two books, and we had many, many discussions about the contents of virtually every chapter of the other books, and since Chris is a God-given friend, I was very intrigued about how the new chapters were received by him. I honestly had no idea how the book was, or if he would remotely like it as I sent each new chapter to him.

Just one side note: John MacArthur was the keynote speaker for the 2000 ETS convention. I was excited to hear him, especially since my life eternally changed when someone handed me a John MacArthur tape many years before. I became hooked on the Bible and to this day have no desire whatsoever to wiggle off the hook. Of all things, the faculty dinner for the school where I taught had been planned to take place at the same time. Although I very much wanted to hear John MacArthur speak in person (I had only previously met him in a receiving line when I was in seminary), I thought it the better discretion to go to the faculty dinner (which I also enjoyed). I arrived back to the conference in time to hear John say his closing words, which I remember (in paraphrase form) to this day: "When I get to the end of my life and I look back on my ministry, what I want it to be shown is whether I did that or God did that." Those are words I took to heart immediately when I heard them, and they remain with me to this day, especially as God opens more and more opportunities for the books.

For the remainder of November and December 2000, I finished the semester and finished the remaining chapters of *The Stone and the Glory*. I would still send the chapters to Chris Bush as I wrote them, and I would get to interact with him after he read each one. This was such a strange process to me because I still had not read the book. It would not be until after Christmas that I was able to start at the beginning and read through it. I knew it was a rough draft and that there would be many changes and editing work, but for the most part (at the time) the book was finished.

As I look back over writing *The Stone and the Glory*, the process and experience were so different from those with the previous two books. As mentioned, God ministered to me so deeply when I wrote *The Cup and the Glory*, and I worshiped God throughout the writing of *The Darkness and the Glory*. Yet, in writing *The Stone and the Glory*, neither one took place (not that they necessarily have to). I think a large part was because I was trying to complete the rough draft and decided not to go back and read it while I was writing it. I enjoyed the book once I finally got to read it, but it was almost like reading someone else's work because I could not exactly remember what was contained within each chapter.

So, as with the other Glory Books, they sat in my office at home until the proper time. *The Cup and the Glory* was published in March 2006, and I began teaching at The Master's Seminary in August 2006.

Before the publication of *The Cup and the Glory*, as some of you know, I would give it away, "charge" people prayer, and ask them to pass it on to someone they thought needed it. Since publishers had turned down *The Cup and the Glory*, I knew they would not accept *The Darkness and the Glory*. I think I submitted it to maybe one or two publishers, but I had no great plans for how it would be published. Probably ten to fifteen people had read it. John MacArthur would be somewhere around the fifteenth reader of *The Stone and the Glory*.

In the summer of 2009, I still had not received official word the book would be published. As I have written and said many times before, "It's not official until it is official." In other words, I had many times where I thought something was a "sure thing from God" that turned out not to be. I have learned to wait and watch. In August 2009 Betsy and I were able to go on a weeklong vacation. Both of us were able to make small corrections in the manuscript. A couple of days after we returned from vacation, Rick Kress let us know that they were ready to publish the third glory book.

How to Use the Study Guide

*T*he Stone and the Glory is the continuation of *The Cup and the Glory* and *The Darkness and the Glory*. The three books connect with one another in that they all eventually end and focus on the Glory of God. First, if you really want to do your study right, I highly recommend that you read and work through *The Cup and the Glory* and its study guide. (You can order these from the website www.thecupandtheglory.com, as well as listen to or download free related messages where I spoke on the material from the chapters within the book). You can do the same for *The Darkness and the Glory*, www.thedarknessantheglory.com. In essence, if you begin your study with *The Stone and the Glory*, you will be starting in "chapter twenty two" (counting the "His Cup—The Beginning" chapter) of the larger Glory of God studies. Not only will you leave out a great deal of related material, but there will also be many references to both the first book and the study guide throughout this newer book. I realize that for various reasons this will not be possible for some, and you can still study *The Stone and the Glory*, but if you are able to read *The Cup and the Glory* and *The Darkness and the Glory* first, it should be most helpful in this study.

Second, *The Stone and the Glory* is "meat, not milk" (1 Cor. 3:1-2; Heb. 5:12-14); that is, this will be a far deeper study for many of the events related to God's temple and for Jesus Christ's first and second advents. (Group leaders who will be teaching others take note; you may have to walk slowly through certain chapters of the book. You may not be able to cover "a chapter a week" and instead have to divide the chapters at certain points along the way).

It took me a great deal of time to try to write the questions for this study guide in such a way that it would fit the largest audience who will be reading this. I tried to write it as though I was sitting there with a person or a group. Obviously, not all Christians or groups are on the same spiritual level, so it will not affect everyone the same way. As referenced in *The Cup and the Glory Study Guide*, such a wide range exists with those who have additional reading materials (such as commentaries or study Bibles) to do follow-up studies, as well as with those who have different spiritual levels, or as those who are a part of a group study. Phrasing a question in such a way that it points people to find the answer in the Word is not the easiest undertaking. I recommend that if you come across a question that you cannot answer at the present time, mark it and come back to it later; it may make a lot more sense after you have read additional material from either the Word or the book.

The format of this study will be the same as that used in *The Cup and the Glory Study Guide*:

1. **Scripture references used.** These refer to the broader context that you can read to get the flow of the Bible verses. The specific references will be given also, although sometimes the chapter will have so many Bible verses that I just refer people back to the chapter to review the Scriptures within it.

2. **Reading assignments.** These will generally be assignments from *The Stone and the Glory*. These are put here as a reminder that the questions should be considered after reading the chapters or the entire book. In fact, many of the questions will make no sense whatsoever unless the chapter has been read.

3. **Questions from *The Stone and the Glory*.** These will be given with page numbers. I hope that these will be useful in either reviewing or contemplating important points.

4. **Questions from the Word.** This section comes directly from the highlighted biblical text of each, with some of the other Scripture passages cited.

5. **The Heart of the Matter.** I put this section in because many people will be doing this study by themselves or in very small groups where they may not have a teacher with them. This section is primarily review, pinpointing the significant "make sure you understand this" points of the chapter, and should cement some of the biblical truths into people's hearts and minds. If you think you have a good handle on the material, you can bypass this section: if you (or your group) cannot answer any of these, you can go back to the previous sections and find the answers.

6. **Personal Application Section.** This is to be used first for your own Christian walk and then in ministering to others. As you will see, this will be set up with a lot of your own interaction with God and His Word.

7. **Deeper Walk Study.** This section takes a little longer. No class, message series, or book ever remotely comes to the "bottom of the mine" in the wonders of God's Word. This section is for those who want to follow the "where do I go from here" for additional biblical truths you can research. As before, these are set up prima rily so that you can do these entirely from the Bible. Of course, any good, solid commentaries will enhance your study.

Just a quick note: as with the study guide for *The Darkness and the Glory*, I did not decide on any daily reading section for the study guide. The "meat, not milk" Bible studies (that is, a deeper Bible study or topic) always take longer to do. I have found since the first book was published that people go at various paces in their studies. I have heard from many, many people who tell me that they have to stop and read a sentence, paragraph, page, or chapter over and over and meditate on it. Sometimes it is a matter of conviction that God is doing in their life as a Christian that makes them want to read at a slower pace; other times it is abject wonder at what God has done for those who are in Christ. I do not want to hinder any such work of the Spirit. I so much would rather God do the timing. For you who want to do daily reading, you could divide the material according to your own pace. Also, *The Stone and the Glory* has many more massive blocks of Scripture than the other two Glory books. You may just want to read through these sections of Scripture on your own and at your on pace, especially once you have finished going through the book and the study guide.

I very much hope this next part will be a fruitful study unto the Glory of God.

To God be the Glory!

Greg Harris
August 2009
The Master's Seminary

1

The Stone

When I pastored in College Park, Maryland, we spent years studying First Peter. It was the first book I was privileged to preach through, although when I left the church we had barely completed chapter three, and obviously had not reached the end of this beloved epistle.

What eventually became "The Lesson" (chapter seven in the book) was actually the first part of my study for what would eventually become *The Stone and the Glory*. (Why this chapter was later divided into two sections will be explained in the introduction section of those chapters). The multiple uses of "Stone" in reference to Jesus in First Peter 2:4-8 intrigued me. By this time I was a much more careful student of the Word in the sense of asking, especially with Old Testament quotes, "Why did God use this reference? What was the context for each Scripture reference? Is this quoted only here, or does it occur elsewhere in Scripture?" One of my most worshipful studies was tracing the Stone references that Jesus used during the week of His last Passover with eternally crucial matters relating to both His death and return. We will get there in chapters seven and eight.

So, knowing that the Stone references were so essential to the Messiah's work, both past and present, I thought it would be a good idea to trace this through Scripture. I wanted to see where it was first used in the Bible, and then follow the trail to the Gospels and First Peter. I had no idea if there would be anything or not and was thrilled to find (as usual) there was so much more God had given in His Word than I had realized.

Also, since the Stone reference used by Jacob/Israel in Genesis 49:23-24 was when he was an older man with not long to live, I wanted to see if there were any other Stone references used either by him or by God. Hopefully, you will see the necessity of "working backwards" from the Genesis 49 reference in order to gain a fuller perspective.

This chapter and these verses are so vital in our understanding of the work of the Lord in our lives as individuals, in past history, and in many prophecies yet to be fulfilled. This will become more evident as we study each additional chapter.

SCRIPTURE REFERENCES

Key passages used in this chapter include: Genesis 25:19-26, Genesis 27, Genesis 49:23-24, and John 4.

READING ASSIGNMENTS

Read chapter one "The Stone" before attempting to answer any of the following questions.

QUESTIONS FROM THE STONE AND THE GLORY

1. Why is the account of "Jacob's Ladder" (Gen. 28:12-15) a great display of God's grace and covenant faithfulness instead of being a reward for Jacob (pp. 17-19)? Explain.

    _____

    _____

    _____

    _____

2. How do the contents of Jacob's two prayers recorded in Genesis 28:20-22 and 32:9-12 show his growth in his spiritual maturity? Show this by listing some of the specifics in his prayers and by his actions (pp. 19-21).

    _____

    _____

    _____

    _____

3. What can we learn about Jesus and His being at the well before the Samaritan woman arrived, plus how He lovingly led her to salvation (pp. 22-28)? Explain.

    _____

    _____

    _____

    _____

4. What can we learn about the woman at the well from before she met Jesus, to her initial encounter with Him, and how she grew to trust Him, even at the beginning stages of her spiritual walk (pp. 22-28)? Give details in how she progressed in her understanding and faith.

    _____

    _____

    _____

    _____

5. Who are the three seekers in John 4? Why is each one important? Explain (pp. 28-30).

_____

_____

_____

_____

*T*he account of John 4 indicates that Jesus was sitting alone by the well (John 4:6)—but this was not just any well in the region. Jesus sat at *the* well. John revealed vital details for understanding much of the conversation that would follow: "So He came to a city of Samaria called Sychar, near the parcel of ground that Jacob gave to his son Joseph; and Jacob's well was there. So Jesus, being wearied from His journey, was sitting thus by the well. It was about the sixth hour" (John 4:5-6). This is the same well that Jacob had given to Joseph back in Genesis 48:22, and this is the context from which Jacob attested to "the God who has been my shepherd all my life" (Gen. 48:15). The well was functional because it supplied water, but beyond that, this was a well of Samaritan history and pride. Although the Jews disdained the Samaritans (and the Samaritans the Jews), the Samaritans were quite proud of their ancestral lineage. This well was their Plymouth Rock; Jacob's well was their heritage.

Here the Shepherd stations Himself. Jesus sits alone by Jacob's well of stone, not many yards away from where Jacob had made an altar to Him, naming it "God, the God of Israel." Here Jesus waits for the lamb who will unexpectedly encounter Him, much in the same way her ancestor Jacob unexpectedly experienced his life-changing encounter with God almost nineteen hundred years earlier.

—*The Stone and the Glory*, p. 22

QUESTIONS FROM THE WORD

1. In Genesis 25:19-34 list several important matters related to the birth of Esau and Jacob, especially noting the specific statements and declarations of God (pp. 14-17).

_____

_____

_____

_____

2. What is the importance of Genesis 27 (pp. 16-17)? How does Jacob show his desire for blessing, yet show his lack of trust in God as seen in his actions? Explain.

_____

_____

_____

_____

3. What is the significance of Genesis 12:1-2, 28:12-15, and Romans 9:10-13 as it relates to God's promises (pp. 17-19)? Explain.

_____

_____

_____

_____

4. What is the importance of Shechem as it relates to Genesis 33:18-20, 48:22, Joshua 24:1, and John 4:6 (pp. 20-21). Explain.

_____

_____

_____

_____

5. Based on the previous questions from this section, list several factors of importance from John 4 (pp. 25-28). These will become very important in the study for the remainder of the book.

_____

_____

_____

_____

*J*esus had originally asked the woman to, "Give me a drink," but He never got one. The woman left her water pot as she raced back to the village. Still, Jesus was more than content with the outcome. He actually had given water—and life eternal—to one who needed it much more than He needed physical refreshment.

She would never be an outcast again; she would never be alone. Even in the future as she walked the path to the well, each trip would vividly remind her of the Shepherd she had so unexpectedly encountered there. Her water vessel even looked different, and she could never consider it totally empty again, for it would become a constant reminder of the day that she received the Water of Life. Since John recorded that many of the Samaritans first believed because of her word (4:39), and then later because of the words of Jesus, many more believed (4:41), she also picked up a new family of faith who likewise drank the from the Savior's spring. The Good Shepherd likely would have divinely nudged other newborn sheep to walk alongside this first Samaritan lamb in rejuvenating sisterhood.

She came to the well that day an outcast among outcasts. She ran back to her village a princess.

— *The Stone and the Glory*, p. 28

THE HEART OF THE MATTER

Before moving on to the next section, you should be able to answer the following questions. If you are unable to answer the following questions biblically, study the appropriate sections again. (Remember: this section is intended only for review).

1. Why is the account of "Jacob's Ladder" (Gen. 28:12-15) a great display of God's grace and covenant faithfulness instead of being a reward for Jacob (pp. 17-19)?

2. What is the importance of Shechem as it relates to Genesis 33:18-20, 48:22, Joshua 24:1, and John 4:6 (pp. 20-21)?

3. What can we learn about the woman at the well from before she met Jesus, to her initial encounter with Him, and how she grew to trust Him, even at an early stage (pp. 22-28)?

4. Who are the three seekers in John 4? Why is each one important (pp. 28-30)?

PERSONAL APPLICATION SECTION

1. How was God's revelation of Himself an act of divine grace? Why did Jacob not deserve this? How similar is this grace to your own salvation experience in God's saving you? Explain this to someone else.

_____

_____

_____

_____

2. How does Jesus show grace in stationing Himself at the well (John 4:6) before the woman arrived? What does this show you about Jesus? What does this show you about the sovereignty of God? How does this relate to your own life? Explain.

_____

_____

_____

_____

3. How does Jesus lovingly "grow" the woman at the well with His patient encounter with her? Explain. How has He done so with you as well? List some examples and thank God for these.

_____

_____

_____

_____

4. How do the three seekers in John 4 relate to you personally in your initial salvation experience, your current walk, and in worshiping God? Explain.

_____

_____

_____

_____

5. Write your own personal application question from this chapter (in other words, "what have I learned") that was not asked elsewhere and give the answer to your question.

_____

_____

_____

_____

*H*ow arduous it must have been during biblical times for mothers with small children or infants to travel up to one hundred miles or more on donkey or on foot. As the Jewish mothers no doubt used to encourage their weary and impatient children on their pilgrimage to Jerusalem, "Hush, child! We are not there yet. We have a ways to go. Settle down. Be patient. It will be worth it when we arrive. We are going to the Holy City of God"—the same holds true for us. But we have work to do. We must drop down into the Word "to see with their eyes and hear with their ears" the events and truths that God reveals. As always, God's Word contains marvelous mysteries and markers that God Himself has set before us. But we must be good Bible detectives. Expressed in another way, we are mining for gold from God's gold mine—not only with Divine permission, but also with Divine delight. Mining for riches, however, takes careful consideration and sifting. In order for us to worship God in spirit and truth, we need to know—and sift through—some biblical history and chronology, and recognize a gold nugget when we see one.

Behold! The life-giving Shepherd is at the well—and He still speaks to us today.

Behold! If we knew the gift of God and Who is speaking, we, too, would run to the well, and then away from it to tell others.

Behold! God has set forth His Stone all throughout Scripture for us to see.

After all, the Father still seeks—presently seeks—worshipers to worship Him in spirit and truth. And He passionately desires for us to know, love, and worship the Shepherd, the Stone of Israel—Whom God Himself selected.

—*The Stone and the Glory*, pp. 29-30

DEEPER WALK STUDY

For those who want to research additional related Scripture and topics, consider the following:

Trace the accounts in more detail by:

(1) Reading Genesis 12, 15, 17, 27–49 noting and specifically listing God's promises and faithfulness.

(2) Reading John 4 and listing items in the account that show God's grace and faithfulness, especially noting those that harmonize with Genesis 27-49.

2

The Place

*I*n doing my "sketchpad study," that is, the framework of the study, the subtitle of the book is usually the last thing that I do. Often I do not know where the studies are going, and it is only after many chapters are written that I can go back and read them and see if there are common elements in them. I am not trying to force them; I am trying to see if they exist.

"The Place" was one of those chapters. It started in John 4:20 with the statement by the Samaritan woman regarding "the place." Then I went through the Bible and started noticing some of the key instances where God Himself referred to "the place." As you will see in this chapter, the phrase "the place" does indeed show up in numerous sections of Scripture, and they are very significant ones. It is also worthy to note that in these passages there is an enormous distinction between "places" and "place," which is the point of the chapter.

This is somewhat of a hinge chapter, but it is a necessary one. It lays foundational truths that we will come back to in the upcoming chapters.

SCRIPTURE REFERENCES

Key passages used in this chapter include: Genesis 22, 1 Chronicles 21-22, and 2 Chronicles 3.

READING ASSIGNMENTS

Read chapter two "The Place" before attempting to answer any of the following questions.

QUESTIONS FROM THE STONE AND THE GLORY

1. What was the origin of the Samaritans, and why would the Jews hate them so? How does this background help you understand the basis of what the Samaritan woman said to Jesus in John 4:20? Explain (pp. 33-34).

_____

_____

_____

_____

2. What is significant about the place Moriah? What is the significance of its name? Explain (pp. 34-36).

_____

_____

_____

_____

3. How did David act foolishly in conducting the census? How did he act wisely once he was confronted with his sin (pp. 35-36)?

_____

_____

_____

_____

4. How does God's dealing with David connect with the Genesis account? Explain (p. 40).

_____

_____

_____

_____

5. What are some of the significant truths concerning the only two places in the Bible where the name Moriah appears (pp. 40-41)?

_____

_____

_____

_____

God had chosen Moriah for this divinely mandated sacrifice. The name Moriah is appropriate for the place where God sent Abraham. Lost in translation are sublime biblical nuances, almost puns of the original language. Moriah is a combination of three Hebrew words meaning, "the place," plus the verb "to see," and finally the "Yah" of Yahweh. *Moriah: the place to see God.* Yet, even beyond this, the word can be translated (with a few subtle changes to the root words) with either an active voice or a passive voice, with different results for each translation. The active voice makes the word mean, "The place where God provides or furnishes." The passive voice renders it, "The place where God appears." Both are correct grammatically; both are correct biblically; both factor in with the conversation between Abraham and Isaac.

In a preliminary way, God had indeed "seen" for Himself a sacrifice. Note the connection Abraham made with what God accomplished. Genesis 22:14 states, "Abraham called the name of that place, 'The LORD Will Provide,' as it is said to this day, 'In the mount of the LORD it will be provided.'" This place became both a name and a proverb—and a promise— of God. Moriah: "the place where God appears." Moriah: "the place where God provides." Each translation is accurate, both grammatically and theologically.

— The Stone and the Glory, pp. 35-36

QUESTIONS FROM THE WORD

1. Contrast 2 Chronicles 7:15-16 with 1 Kings 12:25-32 and note the covenant violations that King Jeroboam committed (pp. 31-32).

   _____

   _____

   _____

   _____

2. What did God promise in Genesis 22:7-13? Did He provide what He promised? Explain (pp. 35-36).

   _____

   _____

   _____

   _____

3. What is similar and different about the 2 Samuel 24 and the 1 Chronicles 21 accounts? Why is this important? Explain (pp. 36-39).

   _____

   _____

   _____

   _____

4. How did God sovereignly direct the judgment so that it ended up as a means of grace in 1 Chronicles 21:19-25 (p. 39)? Explain.

   _____

   _____

_____

_____

5. What is the significance of 1 Chronicles 22:1-5 and 2 Chronicles 3:1? Explain what it is and why it is important (pp. 39-41).

_____

_____

_____

_____

---

*Y*et, tucked away, almost without notice, is a one-sentence revelatory nugget that draws the entire account together. Nothing about this episode with David and the census and God's response merely happened haphazardly. God *led* David to the place, leading for three days as God had previously led Abraham for three days. Strategically, God led David to the exact place where He had led Abraham centuries before. Second Chronicles 3:1 uncovers a three-word goldmine: "Then Solomon began to build the house of the LORD in Jerusalem *on Mount Moriah*, where the LORD had appeared to his father David, at the place that David had prepared on the threshing floor of Ornan the Jebusite."

— The Stone and the Glory, p. 40

THE HEART OF THE MATTER

Before moving on to the next section, you should be able to answer the following questions. If you are unable to answer the following questions biblically, study the appropriate sections again. (Remember: this section is intended only for review).

1. What was the origin of the Samaritans, and why would the Jews hate them so, and how does this help you understand the basis of what the Samaritan woman said to Jesus in John 4:20 (pp. 33-34)?

2. What is significant about the place and name Moriah (pp. 34-36)?

3. What is similar and different about the 2 Samuel 24 and the 1 Chronicles 21 accounts, and why is this important (pp. 36-39)?

4. What is the significance of 1 Chronicles 22:1-5 and 2 Chronicles 3:1, and why is it important (pp. 39-41)?

PERSONAL APPLICATION SECTION

Since this is a hinge chapter with what follows, there will not be as much personal application in this section. More will come later.

1. List some of the items from your study in this chapter that show God's sovereignty. How does knowing these truths help your own understanding of God and your life? Explain.

_____

_____

_____

_____

*T*he Samaritans, of which the woman of John 4 was representative, were wrong. God had selected Mount Moriah in Jerusalem—not Shechem in Samaria. Only twice does Moriah appear in the entire Bible: each instance depicts God's specific leading; each time requires God's specified sacrifice at His designated place. Both references look beyond the immediate participants to the greater work of God.

On Moriah: God will prepare (literally, "see") for Himself a lamb (Gen. 22:8).

Abraham named the place "The LORD will provide."

As it is said to this day, both proverbially and prophetically: "On the mountain of the LORD it will be provided" (Gen. 22:14).

— *The Stone and the Glory*, pp. 40-41

DEEPER WALK STUDY

For those who want to research additional related Scripture and topics, consider the following:

Trace the accounts in more detail by:

(1) Reading Genesis 12, 15, 17, 27–49 noting and specifically listing God's promises and faithfulness.

(2) Reading John 4 and listing items in the account that show God's grace and faithfulness, especially noting those that harmonize with Genesis 27-49.

3

The Dwelling

*T*his section of the book is bitter sweet in many ways. Throughout the Bible God gives many examples of His original design followed by the sinful folly of sin, followed by judgment—but quite often judgment tempered by divine mercy and grace. For instance, the creation glories of God's original design in Genesis 1-2 follow shortly in Genesis 3 with the sin, the fall, and the curse. How different life would be for us if we presently lived under the blessedness of Genesis 1-2.

The same would be true for the ratification of the Mosaic Covenant (Exod. 24), immediately followed by God's desire and design to dwell in the midst of His people (Exod. 25). God's original design, however, was followed by the high-handed sin of the golden calf rebellion (Exod. 32), resulting with God's removing His presence from the camp because of their sin (Exod. 33). Nevertheless, God consecrated His own tabernacle with His glory (Exod. 40), and then later again with His own Temple (2 Chron. 7:1-3). Yet, as you have read or will read in this chapter, the nation repeatedly and horrendously sinned, and God ultimately removed His glory from His Temple.

God chose to remove His glory from His Temple, *but* He did not choose to remove His promises for the future. As we shall see in the upcoming chapters, many, many promises of God must be fulfilled. In fact, His judgments that He promised and executed are so precise we should expect the same precision with the future promised blessings of Yahweh.

SCRIPTURE REFERENCES

There are too many key Scripture references in this chapter to emphasize just a few. You may want to highlight them in your book as you read, or jot them down in the study guide.

READING ASSIGNMENTS

Read chapter three "The Dwelling" before you attempt to answer any of the questions.

QUESTIONS FROM THE STONE AND THE GLORY

1. What is the significance of the "forever" promises made in the Abrahamic Covenant (p. 43)? Why is this important? Explain.

_____

_____

_____

_____

2. What are some factors that show God's mercy and grace in giving the law (pp. 44-46)? Explain.

_____

_____

_____

_____

3. Based on the previous expulsion by God of Adam and Eve in Genesis 3:22-24, why would the promise that God would dwell in the very midst of the people be so stunning (p. 45)? Why is this a grace act of God? Explain.

_____

_____

_____

_____

4. Why would the promise of God to consecrate His tabernacle with His glory be so unexpected based on everything else that had happened from Genesis up to this point (pp. 46-47). Explain.

_____

_____

_____

_____

5. What does Solomon reveal about his father David's intentions to build a Temple for God (pp. 49-50)? Explain.

_____

_____

_____

_____

6. What can we learn about God's faithfulness and holiness from Solomon's prayer at the Temple dedication (pp. 49-51)? Why is this important? Explain.

_____

_____

_____

_____

7. What is the importance of God's removing His glory from His Temple before it fell (pp. 54-55)? Explain.

_____

_____

_____

_____

God then gave directions concerning something that had never been done before in the history of His creation: "Let them construct a sanctuary for Me, that I may dwell among them. According to all that I am going to show you, as the pattern of the tabernacle and the pattern of all its furniture, just so you shall construct it" (Exod. 25:8-9). For the first time since the expulsion of Adam and Eve from His presence in Genesis 3, God Himself would dwell in the very midst of His creation. This was totally God's idea—and highly unexpected.

Once the people had arrived at Mount Sinai and God's glory descended on it, the young nation responded in abject fear, terror, and dread to this small display of God's power (Deut. 5:22-27; Heb. 12:18-21). Yet, to dwell in the very midst of the people He had redeemed was God's desire and His intent. However, certain essential elements had to be addressed. For instance, God is holy—mankind is not. How can a holy God dwell in the midst of a sinful people? How can a holy God be approached in holiness if there are no holy humans on earth? God realized this; consequently, the heart of His earthly abode was to be the means for the atonement of sin.

—*The Stone and the Glory*, p. 45

QUESTIONS FROM THE WORD

1. What are some of the differences between the Abrahamic Covenant (Gen. 12, 13, and 15) and the Mosaic Covenant (Exod. 24) (pp. 43-45)? Explain.

_____

_____

_____

_____

2. What is the significance of the Law/Mosaic Covenant being ratified (Exod. 24:4-8), immediately followed by a promise from God to dwell among His people (Exod. 25:8-9)? Why did the Mosaic Covenant have to be ratified (i.e., "officially started") before God made this promise? Explain (pp. 45-47).

_____

_____

_____

_____

3. What is the significance of God's sanctuary having a mercy seat (Exod. 25:17-21)? What did God promise to do there? Why was this important? Explain (pp. 45-47).

_____

_____

_____

_____

4. What is the importance of Exodus 40:34-38? How is this similar to 2 Chronicles 7:1-3? What are some of the major points to consider about God's glory being inside the Holy of Holies? Explain (pp. 47-49).

_____

_____

_____

_____

5. Why was the three-step removal of God's glory both majestic and sad (pp. 52-53)? Explain.

_____

_____

_____

_____

6. Just prior to the final phase of God's removing His glory, He made specific promises in Ezekiel 11:16-20. What are these promises and why are they even more emphasized

in that He gave them just before He removed His glory? Explain (p. 53).

_____

_____

_____

_____

7. What is the eternal importance of 2 Chronicles 7:12-16? Explain (pp. 54-55).

_____

_____

_____

_____

*E*ven though Scripture later reveals, "The heavens are declaring the glory of God" (Ps. 19:1), and the seraphim of Isaiah 6:1-3 call out to one another, "Holy, Holy, Holy, is the LORD of hosts, the whole earth is full of His glory," the curse of Genesis 3 affected everyone—and every thing (Rom. 8:18-22). Centuries later, the beloved Apostle John wrote —even after Jesus had ascended into heaven—"the whole earth lies in the power of the evil one" (1 John 5:19). The putrid defilement of sins' effects did not begin at these passages such as Romans 8 or 1 John 5:19, or even with the demonic hierarchy disclosed in Ephesians 6:12; they are simply revealed in these passages. They came into existence immediately as part of the consequences of the fall and the resulting curse.

This is why Exodus 29:43 ("And I will meet there with the sons of Israel, and it shall be consecrated by My glory") is so stunningly extraordinary. Since the expulsion of the newly defiled couple from God's garden and presence in Genesis 3, God Himself not only promised to dwell among His people—but even beyond this—one particular place would be consecrated by His own glory. This is the first time in Scripture that God promised this; nowhere else on earth at any time after the fall did God display His special glory presence.

— *The Stone and the Glory*, pp. 46-47

THE HEART OF THE MATTER

Before moving on to the next section, you should be able to answer the following questions. If you are unable to answer the following questions biblically, study the appropriate sections again. (Remember: this section is intended only for review).

1. Based on the previous expulsion by God of Adam and Eve in Genesis 3:22-24, why would the promise that God would dwell in the very midst of the people be so unexpected (p. 45)?

2. What is the significance of the Law/Mosaic Covenant being ratified (Exod. 24:4-8), immediately followed by a promise from God to dwell among His people (Exod. 25:8-9) (pp. 45-47)?

3. Why would the promise of God to consecrate His tabernacle with His glory be so unexpected based on everything else that had happened from Genesis up to this point (pp. 46-47)?

4. What is the importance of God's removing His glory from His Temple before it fell (pp. 54-55)?

5. What is the eternal importance of 2 Chronicles 7:12-16 (pp. 54-55)?

PERSONAL APPLICATION SECTION

1. Many people wrongly see the God of the Old Testament as a "God of hate" and the God of the New Testament as a "God of love." What are some factors that show God's mercy and grace in the instructions for the tabernacle? What can we learn about God from these?

_____

_____

_____

_____

2. Do the same thing as for the question above regarding God's instructions for His Temple.

_____

_____

_____

_____

3. Even in executing God's promised judgments on the nation of Israel, we see His grace, mercy, and faithfulness. What are some examples of these, and what can you learn about God from these? Explain.

_____

_____

_____

_____

4. Write your own personal application question from this chapter (in other words, "what have I learned") that was not asked elsewhere and give the answer to your question.

_____

_____

*A*s Nebuchadnezzar's legions approached Jerusalem like picnic ants given free reign at an outdoors summer feast, God had long since abandoned His previous place of dwelling. Although the structure no doubt looked the same to the inhabitants of Jerusalem and to the Temple gatherers, it was then as different as a living human is from a dead human. Despite its majestic, ornate design and implements, and despite the regular sacrifices and rituals by a functioning priesthood, the Temple of God had now become desolate; God Himself had removed His glory and presence. It was a biblical necessity for God to remove His glory; otherwise, the combined forces of both the human and demonic worlds could never have entered into the Holy of Holies—let alone devour the Temple. If Moses or God's designated priests could not enter into the tabernacle or Temple because of God's glory, how much less could pagan barbarians putrefied in their own vileness approach the Holy One? God's glory had departed, and all that remained of the Temple was a vacant stone shrine of no lasting value. Long before the first Babylonian foot soldier approached the outermost sanctions of God's Temple, God had extracted every semblance and evidence of His previous abode—with one major exception. In spite of His absence, and in a mysterious way, God was uniquely present in His Temple.

—The Stone and the Glory, p. 54

DEEPER WALK STUDY

For those who want to research additional related Scripture and topics, consider the tracing in the following Scripture making key observations, comparisons and contrasts in your reading:

Trace the accounts in more detail by:

(1) Genesis 15 and Exodus 24-25.

(2) Leviticus 26 and Deuteronomy 28.

(3) Second Chronicles 1–7.

(4) Ezekiel 1, 8–11.

4

The Placement

*T*he sovereignty of God is a massive subject, perhaps one of the largest in the Bible. In essence, Genesis through Revelation could accurately be stated as a study on the sovereignty of God.

Usually, especially as baby Christians, we start the study of the sovereignty of God with ourselves, our salvation experience, our circumstances, which is fine to do and no doubt pleasing to God. This is exactly what the Samaritan woman of John 4 did. The reason we start there is that at this point this is pretty much all we know and is part of our testimony. As we "grow in the grace and knowledge" of the Lord Jesus Christ (2 Peter 3:18), we start to learn of—and hopefully appreciate—God's sovereignty as we read His Word. He literally does indeed uphold all things "by the word of His power" (Heb. 1:3).

God's faithfulness is an aspect of His sovereignty because not only does God make promises, but also He minutely brings about what He promises. This is true for both sections of blessing and of judgment. As sad as it is to read about the sins and consequences of someone else, such as the nation of Israel in what people call the Old Testament, we see God repeatedly being true to His Word. This should encourage us regarding God's sovereignty. After all, if God was so precise in executing His promised judgments in the smallest detail, should we not expect the same with the many, many promises He has yet to fulfill when He returns to reign?

SCRIPTURE REFERENCES

Some of the Scripture references in this section are Daniel 9:1-2; Jeremiah 25:11-2; Isaiah 44:24–45:7; Haggai 1; Ezra 1 and 3, Zechariah 3.

READING ASSIGNMENTS

Read chapter four "The Placement" before attempting to answer any of the following questions.

QUESTIONS FROM THE STONE AND THE GLORY

1. What was God's role in exiling the Jewish people? What was His role in bringing

them back into the land? Why is this important? Explain (p. 58).

_____

_____

_____

_____

2. What were two visual reminders of the severity of God's judgment for the remnant who returned from the exile (pp. 59-60)? What was His role in bringing them back into the land, and why is this important? Explain.

_____

_____

_____

_____

3. While the Gentile King Cyrus was important on a human level blessing the Jewish people by allowing them to return and rebuild God's Temple, how does God show that He is the real power in bringing this about? Even more so, why is this important (pp. 60-61)?

_____

_____

_____

_____

4. God demanded that His Temple be rebuilt. How did He accomplish this even beyond using the Gentile king (pp. 62-65)?

_____

_____

_____

_____

5. What were the prophecies that God made about His Temple to encourage the builders? Why is it surprising in how He then acted? Explain (pp. 65-66).

_____

_____

_____

_____

6. What two irreplaceable aspects were absent from the rebuilt Temple, and why are these so important and perplexing? Explain (pp. 66-68).

_____

_____

_____

_____

> **D**aniel, an elderly man by the time the events of Daniel 9 transpired, understood from God's Word that the seventy-year period was coming to its completion. *God Himself* would bring a remnant back to Jerusalem. He would use human governments and peoples, but it was God who had exiled the people, God who had determined the length of Jerusalem's desolation, and God who would bring them back into His land. Simply stated, nothing merely happened. Instead, God sovereignly worked in exact accordance with His Word, down to the smallest detail.
>
> As would be expected, so much was different for the Jewish remnant that left Babylon and returned to Jerusalem. The land had been barren and desolate for decades. Grass and weeds and other plants grew where once commerce or legal debate had transpired. Two exceptional visual reminders, though, gave strong evidence of the severity of God's punishment. First was the destruction of the massive city walls that once protected the people from invaders; the rock fragments from its destruction were strewn all over the ancient city. Second, and more important than the first, the beautiful Temple of God no longer existed. Only the charred foundation offered evidence that a once glorious edifice had occupied this spot for over four hundred years. The competing composite emotions for those who returned from Babylon must have been hard to distinguish: relief for the end of the long journey; joy at being home again; deep grief for the desolation of Jerusalem—especially its centerpiece, the Temple; hopelessness that it would not return to the glory in man's eyes to which it once had laid claim.
>
> — *The Stone and the Glory*, pp. 59-60

QUESTIONS FROM THE WORD

1. What was the promise God made in Deuteronomy 28:64-66 (pp. 57-58)? How would these verses eventually apply to the destruction of God's Temple? Explain.

_____

_____

_____

_____

2. What are the two important distinctions about the exile of the Jewish people into Babylon (pp. 58-60)? Why are these important? Explain.

_____

_____

_____

_____

3. How does the return of the nation Israel to the land show God's total sovereignty and precision, especially as seen in Isaiah 44:24–45:7? Why is this important in understand the bigger picture of what was occurring and why? Explain (pp. 60-61).

_____

_____

_____

_____

4. What is the difference in attitudes between David's wanting to build God a temple (2 Samuel 7) with those of the exiles who returned (Haggai 1:1-11)? How does God respond differently to each situation? Explain.

_____

_____

_____

_____

5. How did the foundation of God's rebuilt Temple differ from the first Temple, and why did it evoke such emotion from those who had seen the first Temple (Ezra 3:8-13) (pp. 68-71)?

_____

_____

_____

_____

6. List the "stone prophecies" of Isaiah 8:11-15 and 28:9-16. What do these verses promise, and why are they important? Explain (pp. 68-71).

_____

_____

_____

_____

7. What are God's promises in Zechariah 3:1-9 (pp. 71-73)? Although we will go into these in much more detail in upcoming chapters, just limiting these divine promises

to the original context, why is this reference still so important? Explain.

_____

_____

_____

_____

A segment of Jews had returned home—but not really. They came back to something old, not to something new. They came back to a work in progress, and a hard and arduous work it would be. Everything was different—including them. Israel no longer had a functional kingdom because they had no Davidic Covenant king to reign over them. Humanly speaking, a Gentile world ruler had to grant this conquered remnant permission to return to their own land. When they did return, they were still subject to Gentile powers.

Whether audibly voiced or silently meditated was the likely ever-abiding question: *"Where was God in all this?"*—or perhaps shortened to its base level, *"Where was God?"* These people knew the prophecy of Ezekiel and how the glory of the Lord—and the Lord Himself—had abandoned His Temple. As Ezekiel 11:23 sadly describes, the third and last visible display of God's glory was its brief hovering over the Mount of Olives before disappearing to some place of His choosing. As this group either collectively or individually looked over to the mountain that marked God's exodus from them, would they not feel as orphans—strangers in a strange land that was once their own? Motivation to do anything other than exist must have been in short supply.

—The Stone and the Glory, p. 60

THE HEART OF THE MATTER

Before moving on to the next section, you should be able to answer the following questions. If you are unable to answer the following questions biblically, study the appropriate sections again. (Remember: this section is intended only for review).

1. What are the two important distinctions about the exile of the Jewish people into Babylon (pp. 58-59)?

2. What were two visual reminders of the severity of God's judgment for the remnant who returned from the exile (pp. 59-60)?

3. How does the return of the nation Israel to the land show God's total sovereignty and precision, especially as seen in Isaiah 44:24–45:7 (pp. 60-61)?

4. What two irreplaceable aspects were absent from the rebuilt Temple, and why are these so important and perplexing (pp. 66-68)?

5. What are the "stone prophecies" of Isaiah 8:11-15 and 28:9-16, and why are they important (pp. 68-71)?

PERSONAL APPLICATION SECTION

1. How does God's prophecy about the seventy-year limitation on the first exile show some of His attributes? What are some of these, and what do they teach you about God? Explain.

    _____

    _____

    _____

    _____

2. How does God show His precise care in bringing the nation back to the land (pp. 42-43)? What does this encourage you about other promises in the Bible that have not been fulfilled yet that God has made to believers? Explain.

    _____

    _____

    _____

    _____

3. Write your own personal application question from this chapter (in other words, "what have I learned") that was not asked elsewhere and give the answer to your question.

    _____

    _____

    _____

    _____

*H*ow could anyone ever explain—other than just by the sheer sovereignty of God—that the Jews chose a name for what was inside the Holy of Holies of the second Temple with which God Himself would agree? There was no ark, but there was a Stone. The name for this stone has never changed throughout the centuries. The Jews of Jesus' time called it by the same name. Even Old Testament believing Jews of modern times who hope soon to begin rebuilding the third Temple use the same name for the stone that alone had always resided inside the Holy of Holies on Moriah.

The Jews named this stone on which the ark once stood and later on which the blood was applied when no ark was present, *the Foundation Stone.*

God has too.

But He also named Him Jesus.

—*The Stone and the Glory*, p. 73

DEEPER WALK STUDY

For those who want to research additional related Scripture and topics, consider the following:

Go back through and trace all the Scripture verses used in this chapter and formulate a biblical theology of these verses making careful observations as you read. These chapters are so important for the remaining portion of the book, and the better you understand them, the more that will be to your advantage.

5

The One

*T*hree times in my life I had the privilege of going to Machaerus where John the Baptist was imprisoned and later beheaded. Each time I taught at Jordan Evangelical Seminary, they would be kind enough to obtain a driver and take me there.

The first time I went by myself. The driver stayed in the parking lot. I walked the fairly long path to the ancient ruins alone and had the whole place to myself to investigate at my leisure. I was able to shout and hear the multiple echoes ricochet off mountains. It was one of the best echo producing places I had ever been. I got to see Machaerus, investigate it at my leisure, and appreciate the view, but at this first visit, I was not working on the studies for this book.

The second time I went, I had Chris Bush (of "The Writing of *The Stone and the Glory*" section) with me. I was now working on the content for *The Stone and the Glory*, although Chris did not know it at the time, and I could appreciate being at Machaerus so much more. The "where is he?" call would be highly perplexing to Chris. I just smiled.

On the third trip, I had another God-given friend with me, Brad Sewell. It had been a number of years since I had been in Jordan. Again, they took us to Machaerus. On the previous two occasions I or we had had the entire place to myself, so that is what I expected when Brad and I went. Instead, there were many busloads of about two hundred or more Egyptians who had pulled up and visited the site when we did. Unlike the previous trips, it was so crowded and loud on this visit. It really was quite striking at how different the whole setting was. That was my last visit to Machaerus (for the present time).

Looking back on it now I see more and more the sovereign hand of God in allowing me even to be there, and especially to allow me to walk the first trip by myself, not knowing in anyway that it would end up being a chapter in a book. God knew this, of course, and allowed me the high privilege of seeing where the Forerunner ministered, sent his question to Jesus, and eventually went home to be with the Lord. The prison rooms really are just a few yards below the upper part where all the festivities would have occurred. I was able to look out from where John the Baptist would have been, and see by the questions he asked Jesus why he would be perplexed.

SCRIPTURE REFERENCES

Key passages used in this chapter include: Malachi 4:5-6, Luke 1, and Matthew 11.

READING ASSIGNMENTS

Read chapter five "The One" before attempting to answer any of the following questions.

QUESTIONS FROM THE STONE AND THE GLORY

1. Why would it seem only a few weeks instead of over four hundred years between the prophecy of Malachi 4:5-6 and the events of Luke 1 (pp. 75-76)? Why is this important in reference to God and His promises? Explain.

    _____

    _____

    _____

    _____

2. Why are the events associated with the birth of John (the Baptist) so important biblically (pp. 75-78)? Explain.

    _____

    _____

    _____

    _____

3. How would the child named John be different from any other child born at that time (pp. 76-78)? Why is this important? Explain.

    _____

    _____

    _____

    _____

4. How does John's answer to those who inquire about his identity demonstrate that he understood who he was and what he was doing (pp. 79-81)? Explain.

    _____

    _____

    _____

    _____

5. What was Machaerus, and why is it important? Explain (pp. 81-83).

    _____

    _____

6. What is the significance that John asked only about Jesus' identity and not his own? Explain (pp. 83-85).

_____

_____

_____

_____

7. How did Jesus answer John's question in a way uniquely appropriate for John? Explain how Jesus answered and why this is important (pp. 84-86).

_____

_____

_____

_____

8. What is it about Jesus' answer to John the Baptist that is *so* essential in understanding "the Stone prophecies" God gave in Scripture (pp. 84-86)? Explain how Jesus answered and why this is important.

_____

_____

_____

_____

*A*s the infant grew to toddler and then to young child, his wisdom would eventually surpass that of his parents. Soon thereafter, his biblical understanding would surpass the collective wisdom of all of the pious of Israel. Only one thing filled the void actually established by the Holy Spirit's indwelling: consumption of the Word of God. Nothing else in the world allured or attracted him except the constant feeding on the Word—a feeding in a sense that would never diminish or become satiated, but would grow only deeper as he matured. John's feeding was a communal consumption of fellowship, not the mere accumulation of information and knowledge from the double-lipped cup of God's Word abhorrently mingled with religious tradition or philosophy of man. That course was for others, including Saul the Pharisee before he became transformed into a child of God, and then into Paul the Apostle.

The Holy Spirit Himself created a passion and yearning filled only by the Word He Himself had inspired. John not only acquired biblical knowledge, he became—as all of God's true servants must become—transformed into the vessel of use that God intended.

— *The Stone and the Glory*, p. 78

QUESTIONS FROM THE WORD

1. What is the relationship of Malachi 4:5-6 and Isaiah 40:3 to Luke 1:13-17? Why are these important? Explain.

   _____

   _____

   _____

   _____

2. What did the Holy Spirit want to convey about God and the new baby John by means of Zacharias' prophecy in Luke 1 (pp. 76-78)? Why is this important? Explain.

   _____

   _____

   _____

   _____

3. What is the significance of Luke 3:1-2 as it relates to the ministry of John the Baptist (pp. 79-81)?

   _____

   _____

   _____

   _____

4. According to John 1:29-34, how did John know that Jesus was the Messiah (pp. 80-81)?

   _____

   _____

   _____

   _____

5. Why was John the Baptist arrested (Matt. 14:3-5)? How did this differ drastically from his previous years of ministry?

   _____

   _____

   _____

   _____

6. Why would the prophecies of Isaiah 40:1-11 and Malachi 3:1 confuse John (pp. 82-84)? Explain.

_____

_____

_____

_____

*A*nd then, even much more powerful than in his previous walk, a major turning point occurred in John's life. Luke 3:1-2 records, "Now in the fifteenth year of the reign of Tiberius Caesar, when Pontius Pilate was governor of Judea, and Herod was tetrarch of Galilee, and his brother Philip was tetrarch of the region of Ituraea and Trachonitis, and Lysanias was tetrarch of Abilene, in the high priesthood of Annas and Caiaphas, the word of God came to John, the son of Zacharias, in the wilderness." Previously, John had read the Word; now he became a vessel by which God would present His Word to others. Before, the process was outside-in; read and consume. Now it was inside-out; the Word came to John, and he spoke God's holy Word to the nation. This is not some learned activity; this is the sovereign moving of the Mighty One of Israel within a prophetic vessel of His choosing.

—*The Stone and the Glory,* p. 79

THE HEART OF THE MATTER

Before moving on to the next section, you should be able to answer the following questions. If you are unable to answer the following questions biblically, study the appropriate sections again. (Remember: this section is intended only for review).

1. Why would it seem only a few weeks instead of over four hundred years between the prophecy of Malachi 4:5-6 and the events of Luke 1 (pp. 75-76)?

2. Why would the prophecies of Isaiah 40:1-11 and Malachi 3:1 confuse John (pp. 82-84)?

3. What is the significance that John asked only about Jesus' identity and not his own (pp. 83-85)?

4. What is it about Jesus' answer to John the Baptist that is *so* essential in understanding "the Stone prophecies" God gave in Scripture (pp. 84-85)?

PERSONAL APPLICATION SECTION

1. How does God show His faithfulness from Malachi to Luke 1 (pp. 75-78)? What does this teach you personally about God's faithfulness in your own life? Explain.

_____

_____

_____

_____

2. John the Baptist, even before his birth, would be great in the sight of God (Luke 1:15). What qualities did John demonstrate that would show this to be evident in his life? What can we learn from these, and how do they apply to your life—or do they? Explain.

_____

_____

_____

_____

3. If John the Baptist was such a choice vessel of God, why did he receive such harsh treatment? How does this treatment stand at odds with "the prosperity gospel," and how does this relate to your own life? Explain.

_____

_____

_____

_____

4. John the Baptist went to his death without fully understanding what God was doing and why. What can we learn from this? Explain it to someone you know.

_____

_____

_____

_____

*L*ong before Peter penned these verses in his epistles, Jesus had employed them as well in answer to John's question in Matthew 11:6: "And blessed is he who keeps from stumbling over Me" or "is not scandalized"—employing the verb form of the same word *skandalon* that Peter would later write. In the same way that Peter would later be moved by the Holy Spirit to include these verses in his first epistle, Jesus had answered John the Baptist by alluding to the same Isaiah 8:14 passage in reference as to who He is.

However, in answering John the Baptist, Jesus did something eternally monumental: He changed the Stone reference to Himself. "And blessed is he who does not take offense at Me" (Matt. 11:6). The Stone is present, but the Stone is a *"Me,"* not an *"It."* How Jesus said this at the time with whatever accompanying hand gestures, if any, we do not know. But in the Greek the "Me" is in the emphatic form.

— *The Stone and the Glory*, pp. 85-86

DEEPER WALK STUDY

For those who want to research additional related Scripture and topics, consider the following:

Based on Jesus' answer in Matthew 11:6 showing Him to be "the Shepherd, the Stone of Israel" (Gen. 49:24), go back through the book or the Bible to every stone reference and think in terms of the person or work of Jesus. It will (hopefully) change the way that you look at Him and what He did and is about to do. od's grace and faithfulness, especially noting those that harmonize with Genesis 27-49.

6

The Tested

*F*rom my vantage point, the book makes a major shift after Matthew 11:1-6, especially 11:6, where Jesus identifies Himself in reference to the Isaiah passages. Now the prophecy in Genesis 49:24 ("From there is the Shepherd, the Stone of Israel") can be viewed with the person and work of Jesus in mind. Therefore, the many "Stone prophecies" that we have already seen can be viewed as Messianic promises concerning Jesus. Hopefully, this will cause us to consider them with more understanding and clarity, as Jesus originally intended with His answer to John the Baptist.

Also, knowing the prophecies about God's Stone not only helps us look backward to where we have been so far in our studies and see the work of Jesus, but it also helps set the stage for many strategic prophecies regarding the Stone of Israel that we have yet to encounter. I assure you there is much gold ahead in studying matters related to "The Shepherd, the Stone of Israel."

SCRIPTURE REFERENCES

Key passages used in this chapter include: Isaiah 28:6, Zechariah 3, Isaiah 11:1-10, Matthew 4:1-11, and Daniel 2.

READING ASSIGNMENTS

Read chapter six "The Tested" before attempting to answer any of the following questions.

QUESTIONS FROM THE STONE AND THE GLORY

1. What is the significance of Satan being in the vision recorded in Zechariah 3? Why is this important? Explain (pp. 88-90).

   _____

   _____

   _____

   _____

2. What is the importance of "the eyes" in reference to the Stone prophecies (pp. 91-92)? Although this may seem strange from a human perspective, it is theologically important. What does this indicate about the Stone, and why is this important? Explain.

_____

_____

_____

_____

3. Generally speaking, what is the difference in function between the high priest and a regular priest (pp. 91-93)?

_____

_____

_____

_____

4. When viewed with "the Stone prophecies" we have already seen, especially the last one in Zechariah 3, what is so astounding about the temptation of Jesus (pp. 94-95)? Why would Satan go this route in his temptation? Attempt to explain.

_____

_____

_____

_____

5. One of the aspects of Satan's tempting of Jesus was that Satan took Jesus to the pinnacle of the Temple (Matt. 4:5). If Jesus chose to do so, what were some of the things He could have seen (pp. 95-96)? Why are these vital in understanding both His identity and His mission? Explain.

_____

_____

_____

_____

6. Jesus—not Satan—ended the temptation (Matt. 4:10). What does this show in reference to Jesus qualifying as "the tested stone" (Isaiah 28:16), and why is this important (pp. 99-101)? Explain.

_____

_____

_____

_____

*U*nique is this One of whom Zechariah wrote, "He will be a priest on His throne." Priests do not have thrones—kings do. But One coming Priest would have a throne. Furthermore, in the biblical accounts, Jewish kings were not priests; but One coming King would be. Unique to this coming One, He would be Priest and King—and Stone.

God emphasized the Stone prophecy of Zechariah 3 with three instances of Behold! Pay attention! Mark this!

Satan did; every part of it—he had good reason to do so. When—or if, in his mind—the Stone fulfilled these prophecies, Satan and his realm would be demolished. The Tempter had over four hundred years to plot his strategy before the Spirit led the Stone into the wilderness to be tempted by Satan (Matt. 4:1). Four centuries of strategizing and planning by Satan to defile the true High Priest, to short-circuit the King's coronation, to test and tempt Him beyond the entirety of Adam's lineage's testing. But this One was not only linked to Adam, He was the unique Son of God—and Jesus stepped into the arena of intense spiritual battle in order to qualify and to become the Tested Stone of Isaiah 28.

—The Stone and the Glory, p. 93

QUESTIONS FROM THE WORD

1. What is the significance of Jesus having been "born under the law" (Gal. 4:4), especially in reference to His entire life? In other words, Jesus was born and lived under the law (pp. 87-88). How does this make you read the Gospels differently now, or does it? Explain.

_____

_____

_____

_____

2. What is the importance of Zechariah 3:8-10? What does this prophecy promise regarding "the stone I have set before Joshua" (pp. 88-92)? Why is this important? Explain.

_____

_____

_____

_____

3. How does a prophecy given centuries before in Isaiah 11:1-10 help to explain who the Branch is? How does this relate to the prophecy of Zechariah 3:8-10, and why is this

so important? Explain (pp. 88-92).

_____

_____

_____

_____

4. What is amazing about Satan using Psalm 91:11-12 in tempting Jesus (Matt. 4:6) (pp. 94-95)?

_____

_____

_____

_____

5. What is the setting for Daniel 2, and why is it and its explanation important (pp. 96-99)? Explain.

_____

_____

_____

_____

6. Even though the word "stone" is not used in Matthew 4:8-9, how does Daniel 2:44-45 still connect with the temptation? What does God promise about His Stone, and why is it vital in understanding not only Satan's tempting of Jesus, but also the Messiah's future reign? Explain.

_____

_____

_____

_____

Still, we miss something major in this account. Satan took Jesus to the pinnacle of the Temple. Of all places to take Jesus, this was the farthest from the best option for Satan. Some commentators foolishly write that Jesus would have swooned from the dizzying height. That describes us — not Him. Of all places — the pinnacle of the Temple. From there, even in the midst of Satan's temptation, Jesus could look over to Moriah, where He had once stopped Abraham from sacrificing Isaac; (note "the angel of the LORD" in Genesis 22:11, which is a reference to the preincarnate Jesus). To Moriah, where God would provide for Himself a Lamb. To Moriah, where He later appeared to David, designating the exact place where His own Temple would be built. To Moriah, where His own glory once indwelt *the Temple*—and then departed.

Depending on exactly where Calvary is, all that Jesus had to do was to shift His eyes to see the place where He would die. Perhaps He did, but if so, His eyes would go back to the Holy of Holies, where God Himself had set the Foundation Stone; the place where the Foundation Stone, with the attributes of God, ultimately would take away the iniquity of the land in only one day.

—The Stone and the Glory, p. 95

THE HEART OF THE MATTER

Before moving on to the next section, you should be able to answer the following questions. If you are unable to answer the following questions biblically, study the appropriate sections again. (Remember: this section is intended only for review).

1. What is the significance of Satan being in the vision recorded in Zechariah (pp. 88-90)?

2. What is the general difference between a high priest and a regular priest (pp. 91-93)?

3. When viewed with "the Stone prophecies," especially in Zechariah 3, why is it surprising how Satan tempted Jesus (pp. 94-95)?

4. What could Jesus view from the pinnacle of the Temple, if He chose to, and why is this important (pp. 95-96)?

5. What is the significance of Jesus—not Satan—ending the temptation (pp. 99-101)?

*F*our hundred years of satanic plotting. Four hundred years of calculating the best approach. Where Satan was last seen in what is called the Old Testament, in the Stone prophecy of Zechariah 3, is where he began—and ended—his tempting of Jesus. Even with the centuries of preparation, even with the physically weakened Jesus, each element of the temptation could easily have been responded to with, "I AM the Stone." Satan knew He was—and that does not seem to have been the issue. The way he asked, "If you are the Son of God," has more of the inference in Greek of "since you are Son of God." From each element of Satan's temptation emerged another ray of refracted Light of perfection from God's Precious Stone. Each temptation segment by Satan ultimately revealed some additional aspect of Jesus' being and of His ministry. Each temptation actually gave additional credence to the fact that Jesus is the Stone. Jesus ended the temptation at His desired time—and He left the encounter with much more than when He entered.

The Stone He is, was, and always will be. The Tested Stone He had now become, at least to the degree necessary to this time of His life. Drinking His cup completely at Calvary would conclude the final and most grueling testing.

—The Stone the Glory, pp. 100-101

PERSONAL APPLICATION SECTION

1. Satan tempted Jesus by (among other things) taking Him to the pinnacle of the Temple (pp. 95-96). Knowing that He was ultimately enduring this for us (the 40-day fast, the onslaught of the evil one, Calvary), how does knowing what Jesus could have seen from there, if He chose to do so, make you appreciate Him more in reference to your own salvation? Explain.

_____

_____

_____

_____

2. With what you know about Satan last appearing in Zechariah 3 and next showing up in Matthew 4:1-11 with the temptation of Jesus, how does this make you appreciate Jesus more, or does it? Explain why.

_____

_____

_____

_____

3. Write your own personal application question from this chapter (in other words, "what have I learned") that was not asked elsewhere and give the answer to your question.

_____

_____

_____

_____

DEEPER WALK STUDY

For those who want to research additional related Scripture and topics, consider the following:

Carefully go through the verses and their context in all the Scripture passages listed in "The Tested" and write out careful observations as you read. This is a very important chapter in understanding all of the Stone prophecies about Jesus.

7

The Lesson-Part One

*T*his chapter will always be the most special one for me. It actually the beginning point of my studies for what would eventually become *The Stone and the Glory*, although obviously I had no way of knowing that at the time. *The Cup and the Glory* and *The Darkness and the Glory* were not even thought of (in my mind) at the time. I was pastoring a church in College Park, Maryland, and we were going through First Peter. I was intrigued as we came to First Peter 2:4-8 and the multiple "Stone prophecies" that Peter used. I also wondered why the Holy Spirit would prompt him to use these particular verses.

I was particularly interested in Psalm 118 because at that time I knew nothing about it. I wanted to see where else it occurred in Scripture, and it surprised me to find it the number of times that it showed up during the last week of Jesus' life before He was crucified.

Also, I wanted to see what was involved in Luke 22:8 about preparing the Passover. Alfred Edersheim's *The Temple* is the basis for much of the Jewish history and customs I used in my studies. I have referred to my original copy so many times it has pages falling out (a worthy praise for any godly book). So often we read the Bible and try to carry it over immediately into our own world, society, and time, instead of dropping down into the world of the original participants and seeing how they would have understood common sayings and customs of the day. To this day, I try to maintain this same procedure in my studies. I still learn, I still stay amazed at God and His Word, and I will run out of lifetime before I run out treasure.

This was a very worshipful and tearful chapter to write. What masterful omniscience and omnipotence our Lord repeatedly demonstrates in repeatedly referring to Himself in Psalm 118.

SCRIPTURE REFERENCES

Key passages used in this chapter include: Psalm 118, Matthew 21-24, and Luke 22:1-8.

READING ASSIGNMENTS

Read chapter seven "The Lesson — Part 1" before attempting to answer any of the following questions.

QUESTIONS FROM THE STONE AND THE GLORY

1. Why is the "Triumphal Entry" not a good name for Jesus' riding into Jerusalem (pp. 104-106)?

    _____

    _____

    _____

    _____

2. Based on their previous encounter with Jesus, how would Peter, James, and John view the "Triumphal Entry" as no others would? Explain (pp. 104-105).

    _____

    _____

    _____

    _____

3. Why would the religious leaders be so upset at what Jesus asked in Matthew 21:42-46? What was Jesus saying in reference to Himself, and in reference to them (pp. 109-110)?

    _____

    _____

    _____

    _____

4. Why would Jesus' last words in Matthew 23:37-39 seem so strange to those who originally heard them? What did He say, and why is this important? Explain (pp. 110-112).

    _____

    _____

    _____

    _____

5. Why did Jesus not accept the phrase from Psalm 118, "Blessed is He who comes in the name of the Lord?" How do we know He did not accept it, and how does this relate to future events? Explain (pp. 112-113).

    _____

    _____

    _____

    _____

6. Based on the events of the week and on the ceremony itself, why would Jesus send Peter and John to prepare the Passover (Luke 22:8)? What was involved in the preparation? What would Jesus be teaching them by having them do this? Explain (pp. 113-15).

_____

_____

_____

_____

7. How did "the Hallel" (Psalms 113-118) play a vital role in the Passover? How would the Passover meal end? Why would this have been so hard on Peter and John? Explain (pp. 115-16).

_____

_____

_____

_____

*I*n the second parable, Jesus concluded by quoting Psalm 118:22—the same psalm which is the origin of the Hosannas that were repeatedly shouted by the crowds of the previous days. Peter and John would have witnessed this: "Jesus said to them, 'Did you never read in the Scriptures, "The Stone that the builders rejected, this became the Chief Cornerstone; this came about from the Lord, and it is marvelous in our eyes?"'" (Matt. 21:42).

The chief priests and elders understood that Jesus referred to them in both parables and responded to His teaching by seeking to kill Him (Matt. 21:45-46). They likely would have killed Him on the spot, as they would kill Stephen weeks later—if they could have. But they could not. Someone much greater than they controlled the events of this divinely predicted week.

Jesus mentioned no names in His parables. Why then did the chief priests and Pharisees react so violently? Simply put, the opponents of Jesus responded in wrath because they clearly understood what Jesus was claiming: *He Himself* was the cornerstone *placed by God*. This concerned Jesus' origin and mission and answered their initial question of, "By what authority are you doing these things?" (Matt. 21:23)—"by My Father who placed Me here."

—*The Stone and the Glory*, p. 109

QUESTIONS FROM THE WORD

1. How was Psalm 118:25-26 used at the "Triumphal Entry" (Matt. 21:9)? What does it show that the crowd was anticipating? Why would they think this (pp. 105-106)?

_____

_____

_____

_____

2. How did the question regarding Jesus' authority (Matt. 21:23ff.) set the stage for what else Jesus taught? How did Jesus entrap the religious leaders by the very simple question He asked (pp. 107-110)?

_____

_____

_____

_____

3. What is the first use of Psalm 118 in Matthew's Gospel? How does this set the stage for the second use, and why is this important (pp. 107-110)?

_____

_____

_____

_____

4. How does Psalm 118:25-26 relate to the slaying of the Passover lambs? Based on what Jesus had just recently said (Matt. 23:39), what would be reasonable for the people to expect? Explain (pp. 113-15).

_____

_____

_____

_____

5. How did God use Psalm 113-118 to bear witness to His beloved Son at *every* Passover meal observed that night? Explain how and why this is important (pp. 115-16).

_____

_____

_____

_____

*B*ut beyond these additional condemnations, one essential truth emerged above all the rest: Psalm 118 strongly supports the Messianic claims of Jesus of Who the Messiah of Israel is. Whoever the Messiah was, He *had to be initially rejected* before He would reign in order for Scripture to be fulfilled. Not only was the Messiah to be rejected, but also this rejection must come from those in places of religious authority and responsibility. This prophecy was being fulfilled from the very ones repudiating Jesus at that very moment. That hour was the Trinity-ordained time of Jesus' rejection—not His reign—as the Godhead had mandated in eternity past.

Nevertheless, it still made those who rejected Him responsible for their actions (Matt. 21:44).

The chief priests and elders were not only the builders who rejected the Stone, but they were also the ones who opposed God the Father, because God Himself had placed the Stone. *They*—not the Stone—were the ones standing in direct opposition and hostility to God, and they collectively stood condemned by Scripture. Ironically, the rejection of the Stone by the religious leaders did not diminish the claims of Jesus: the stronger the hostile reaction by the leaders, the greater the Messianic substantiation. God's own Word predicted this would—and must—happen, just as it did, and predicted or not, they intended to add their intensified hostility against the Lamb of God who takes away the sins of the world (John 1:29).

—The Stone and the Glory, p. 110

THE HEART OF THE MATTER

Before moving on to the next section, you should be able to answer the following questions. If you are unable to answer the following questions biblically, study the appropriate sections again. (Remember: this section is intended only for review).

1. Why is the "Triumphal Entry" not a good name for Jesus' riding into Jerusalem (pp. 104-106)?

2. Why would the religious leaders be so upset at what Jesus asked in Matthew 21:42-46? What was Jesus saying in reference to Himself, and in reference to them (pp. 109-110)?

3. Why would Jesus' last words in Matthew 23:37-39 seem so strange to those who originally heard them (pp. 110-12)?

4. Why did Jesus not accept the phrase from Psalm 118, "Blessed is He who comes in the name of the Lord"? How do we know He did not accept it, and how does this relate to future events (pp. 112-13)?

5. Why would Jesus send Peter and John to prepare the Passover (Luke 22:8) (pp. 113-15)?

PERSONAL APPLICATION SECTION

1. Why is this chapter entitled "The Lesson"? What lessons have you learned personally that have enhanced your appreciation of Jesus? Explain this to someone.

_____

_____

_____

_____

2. How do you see the perfect sovereignty and precision of God throughout this chapter? Does this make you trust and appreciate the Trinity more? If so, how? Explain.

_____

_____

_____

_____

3. How does Jesus minutely fulfilling Psalm 118:22-29 make you appreciate Him more? Explain in detail what and why.

_____

_____

_____

_____

4. What in this chapter do you most look forward to telling to others? Who are they, and why do you want to tell them?

_____

_____

_____

_____

5. Write your own personal application question from this chapter (in other words, "what have I learned") that was not asked elsewhere and give the answer to your question.

_____

_____

_____

_____

*W*hy did Jesus not accept Israel's praise at the advent of her Messiah? Simply put, He could not have received the praise of Israel at that time because Psalm 118:22 ("the stone which the builders rejected") had not yet transpired, but would culminate in His crucifixion. The people sang and desired Psalm 118:25-26: "O LORD, do save [Hosanna!], we beseech You; O LORD, we beseech You, do send prosperity! Blessed is the one who comes in the name of the LORD!" But such prophesied days of blessing could not come without first having the builders reject the Stone placed there by God Himself. The times of blessing could not come unless the Lamb of God made proper atonement for the sin of the world (John 1:29). Most of those in Israel—especially the various religious groups—saw no need for such atonement; after all, they had the functioning Temple sacrifices. Jesus never permitted these basest of needs to leave His thoughts.

Jesus had not participated in the Triumphal Entry—only a preview. The true Triumphal Entry awaits Him.

"For I say to you, from now on you shall not *see* Me *until* you say, 'Blessed is He who comes in the name of the LORD'" (Matt. 23:39). Obviously, Jesus' declaration is not a total abandonment of the nation of Israel. One day God will pour out His Spirit on the Jewish people so that they will deeply mourn the One whom they rejected. One day Israel will see: "And it will come about in that day that I will set about to destroy all the nations that come against Jerusalem. And I will pour out on the house of David and on the inhabitants of Jerusalem the Spirit of grace and of supplication, so that they will *look on Me* whom they have pierced; and they will mourn for Him, as one mourns for an only son, and they will weep bitterly over Him, like the bitter weeping over a firstborn" (Zech. 12:9-10). One day, centuries yet in the future from Christ's days on earth, Israel will again sing Psalm 118 at the advent of Jesus. But next time, He will readily accept what has been rightfully His from the beginning. The next pouring forth of praise will be after the cleansing of the nation—and the cleansing of the nations. The next time, Jesus will enter Jerusalem in full Transfiguration glory (Matt. 25:31)—and on a white horse (Rev. 19:11).

—*The Stone and the Glory*, pp. 111-112

DEEPER WALK STUDY

For those who want to research additional related Scripture and topics, consider the following:

Read through Psalms 113–118 making careful observations as you do. Then read Matthew 21–27 and note how important these psalms are and how they factored into the events of that week.

Also, you may want to go to any reference to the Passover in the Gospels and read them with Psalms 113–118 in mind because these psalms would be used with them as well.

8

The Lesson Part 2

*J*ames 3:1-2a warns, "Let not many of you become teachers, my brethren, knowing that as such we will incur a stricter judgment. For we all stumble in many ways." Anyone who takes these verses seriously understands what a serious responsibility that teaching others the Bible is because we all do indeed stumble in many ways. If nothing else, we stumble in our limited understanding of all of God's Word. We also stumble in knowing what the Bible says, yet no one other than Jesus ever remotely did this perfectly. Part of the reason that James 3 addresses teachers is that teachers multiply what they teach. If this is sound doctrine and biblically true, this is wonderful; if this is false doctrine and unedifying, the multiplication effects can be massive—and horrendous.

"The Lesson" was originally written as one chapter. However, in doing additional research and studies, I realized that I was wrong in that I had lumped all the Passover observers on one night instead of two different nights. Once I saw this, I immediately added "The Lesson—Part 2," not only because I will gladly change anything I have written, taught, or preached, but also I absolutely rejoice in the fact that this was not published until I knew about the two side-by-side sacrifices of the Passover lambs.

As I write this study guide, I will be beginning my fourth year at The Master's Seminary in the fall. Because I am on faculty there, many people think that I (or we as faculty members) "have arrived" in our studies or learning. While obviously we have learned much more than we knew at the beginning, it is an on-going learning process for all of us—myself at the forefront. I think I have learned more personally and grown more spiritually since I have arrived at TMS—if in nothing else—just by being in contact beginning with John MacArthur and going all the way down the ladder to the godly people who work in the different support services. Being on faculty there gives me a front row seat for some of the godliest people I have ever met, and many of these happen to be some of the most brilliant Christian minds that God has blessed His church with.

When working through the content for this chapter, I had weekly contact with Dr. Robert Thomas, the one mentioned in the dedication section of this study guide. Quite similar to the scene with the woman at the well and Jesus in John 4, I asked, "Dr. Bob, so which day was right about sacrificing the Passover lambs?" He chuckled and answered, "I guess it depends on who you would have asked?"

That did it for me. I understood exactly what he was talking about and how this fit together. I also thanked God again for restraining this from being published until I could address this very important section.

SCRIPTURE REFERENCES

Key passages used in this chapter include: Exodus 12:1-6, Leviticus 25:1-5, Numbers 9:1-6, Luke 22:7-9, and John 18:28 and 19:14.

READING ASSIGNMENTS

Read chapter eight "The Lesson—Part 2" before attempting to answer any of the following questions.

QUESTIONS FROM THE STONE AND THE GLORY

1. In order for God to accept His Passover, what two requirements did He demand? Why is this important? Explain (pp. 119-22).

    _____

    _____

    _____

    _____

2. In giving the Passover instructions, God repeatedly spoke of a place to establish His name forever (e.g., Deut. 16:5-6). Though not discussed in this chapter, from what we have already seen in our studies, how do these commands relate to the requirements for any future Passovers? Explain (pp. 119-22).

    _____

    _____

    _____

    _____

3. To many people, what seems to be a contradiction in the Bible regarding when the Passover lambs were killed and the feast observed? What is the answer to this dilemma? Explain (pp. 122-24).

    _____

    _____

    _____

    _____

4. Connected with the question above, but so important in understanding the events that follow, which geographical areas and religious groups began their day at what

times? In other words, how would the Pharisees calculate time, and how would the chief priests and Sadducees (pp. 122-24)?

_____

_____

_____

_____

5. What do scholars know and not know about the two different days for sacrificing the Passover Lambs (pp. 123-25)?

_____

_____

_____

_____

6. For those who were about to sacrifice their Passover lambs, what was the dilemma caused by the unexplained darkness? Explain (pp. 125-26).

_____

_____

_____

_____

7. How would the earthquake that occurred totally ruin most, if not all, of the Passover preparations for those who had not yet observed the Feast? Why is this important in their standing before God? Explain (pp. 126-28).

_____

_____

_____

_____

8. Based on what we have studied, what would be interesting if we could witness Annas and Caiaphas observe their next Passover, regardless of when that was? Why (pp. 130-31)?

_____

_____

_____

_____

*A*s we have seen in previous studies, the darkness covered the land from about noon until about 3:00 PM (Matt. 27:45; Mark 15:33; Luke 23:44). Luke added the additional detail of "the sun being obscured" (23:45)—or literally in the Greek, "the sun failing." You can read more about this in "The Darkness" chapter of *The Darkness and the Glory*.

Think what pandemonium must have occurred once this totally unexpected darkness appeared and resided for three hours, especially for the remaining third of the population who had prepared for and had expected to gather at God's Temple and sacrifice their Passover lambs that day. Not only did they have no explanation for the reason the darkness was there in the first place, but also at that time they had no basis for knowing how long it would last. Especially for those who calculated the days from sunset to sunset and had not yet sacrificed their Passover lambs at the Temple, such astounding events would profoundly confuse them. These people told time daily by the sun, and yet such darkness had *never* happened before. They would not have seen the sun traveling its customary course to sunset, accompanied by the expected awe-inspiring sunset hues. The sun had been high in the sky, but then most unexpectedly it had become completely dark. Also, if literally in the Greek "the sun [was] failing" (Luke 23:45), it would certainly follow that the full moon of Passover was also hidden (if it could have been viewed at that time of the day), as were any subsequent stars. These who had always calculated the new day by the advent of sunset must have thought, "*What* day is it? Did we miss the Passover? *How* could we possibly have missed it?" Also, if it were now the "next day," then they *all* had missed the God-ordained sacrificing of the Passover lambs, and by God's Holy Law they would have to wait a month in order to participate in the next one. Furthermore, the extremely strong warning from God in Numbers 9:13 would weigh heavily on anyone who feared Yahweh: "But the man who is clean and is not on a journey, and yet neglects to observe the Passover, that person shall then be cut off from his people, for he did not present the offering of the LORD at its appointed time. That man shall bear his sin." Could it be possible that this promised curse resided on them? Were they to be cut off from God's people? Would they themselves bear the weight of their own sin?

—*The Stone and the Glory*, pp. 125-26

QUESTIONS FROM THE WORD

1. What can we learn from Exodus 12:1-6, Leviticus 23:1-5 and Numbers 9:1-5 about when the Passover lambs were to be sacrificed? Why is this important (pp. 119-21)?

    _____

    _____

    _____

    _____

2. What does Deuteronomy 16:1-5 indicate about any future Passovers regarding both God's name and His designated place? Explain (pp. 119-21).

    _____

    _____

_____

_____

3. What is the significance of God's additional instructions in Numbers 9:6-12? What does Numbers 9:13 demonstrate regarding how God viewed anyone who could have observed but did not observe His Passover? What did God say the punishment was? Explain (pp. 122-24).

_____

_____

_____

_____

4. How does Numbers 9:6-13 help explain the urgency of the Jewish leaders as seen in John 18:28? Explain (pp. 123-24).

_____

_____

_____

_____

5. How did Matthew 27:50-53 change everything that day? What happened, and why is this important? Explain (pp. 126-27).

_____

_____

_____

_____

6. How did God use Psalm 118 to show His utter sovereignty over everyone at Passover, regardless of when it was observed? Explain (pp. 131-33).

_____

_____

_____

_____

*W*hat frantic scurrying there must have been as the remaining masses laboriously made their way in engulfing darkness to sacrifice their Passover lambs in the Temple. What agitation the priests and Levites must have experienced as they would have attempted to answer the countless questions they knew would come, while at the same time trying to execute everything in accordance with the Law. Yet, they, too, must have wondered why the darkness had occurred, and—since they calculated time by sunset—must have pondered whether this was the beginning of the new day. Had these who had been so thoroughly and meticulously trained in the Torah and who had been an active part of dozens of ritualistic slayings of previous years somehow have missed the Passover? Being strict observers of the Law, they would have known that God had set the requirement of where and when the Passover lambs were to be slaughtered, namely, "between the twilights." But at that time, there were no twilights like those on normal days. Many priests and Levites hastily convened, and heated discussions must have erupted about whether or not they should even attempt to fulfill their divinely-mandated priestly and Levitical duties—and they would not have had the option to debate this in the normal, leisurely academic manner. Two pressing questions obviously stood before them: first, what day was it, Passover or the day after it; and second, should they attempt to proceed with the ceremony in the dark? We will find out in heaven how they must have attempted to complete the most critical preparation of the Passover, namely, the designated sacrificing of the Passover lambs. Yet, not one time in history had they or any of their ancestors attempted to do that in the midst of total darkness. Even if the Levites had carried torches, they must have repeatedly bumped into one another and have been greatly hindered in their preparations, especially with something so delicate as the cutting of the sacrificial lambs' throats with the very sharp knives used by those attending.

—*The Stone and the Glory*, p. 126

THE HEART OF THE MATTER

Before moving on to the next section, you should be able to answer the following questions. If you are unable to answer the following questions biblically, study the appropriate sections again. (Remember: this section is intended only for review).

1. What can we learn from Exodus 12:1-6, Leviticus 23:1-5 and Numbers 9:1-5 about when the Passover lambs were to be sacrificed, and why is this important (pp. 119-21)?

2. What does Deuteronomy 16:1-5 indicate about any future Passovers regarding both God's name and His designated place (pp. 119-21)?

3. To many people, what seems to be a contradiction in the Bible regarding when the Passover lambs were killed and the feast observed? How is this easily answered (pp. 122-24)?

4. How would the earthquake that occurred totally ruin most of the Passover preparations for those who had not yet observed the Feast? Why is this important in their standing before God (pp. 126-27)?

5. What happened in Matthew 27:50-53, and why is this important (pp. 126-27)?

6. Based on what we have studied, what would be interesting in witnessing Annas and Caiaphas observe their next Passover, regardless of when that was? Why (pp. 130-31)?

PERSONAL APPLICATION SECTION

1. Consider: God referred to the Jewish feast as "the LORD'S Passover" (Exod. 12:11), not the people's Passover (p. 119). Most people did not historically or do not presently consider the Passover to be the LORD'S Passover. What is the significance of starting with Him and not ourselves? What can we learn about this in our own walk with Him? Explain.

_____

_____

_____

_____

2. In what ways does God show His sovereign control over even His enemies throughout this chapter? List some of them. What does this teach you about God's power and sovereignty? How does this encourage you in your own life? Explain to someone else.

_____

_____

_____

_____

3. Write your own personal application question from this chapter (in other words, "what have I learned") that was not asked elsewhere and give the answer to your question.

_____

_____

_____

_____

*W*hether that same night, or whenever they eventually celebrated Passover, God still bore witness to these two hearts of stone, forcing them to recite the very words that Jesus had asked the authorities if they had ever read: "The stone which the builders rejected has become the chief corner stone. This is the LORD'S doing; it is marvelous in our sight" (Ps. 118:23). Annas and Caiaphas could not have failed to make the connection, for their intensely hated enemy Jesus had put His very own words in their mouths. How interesting it would have been to have watched their growing revulsion as those two of high priestly office further quoted what the multitudes had sung in the presence of Jesus, and what He said must be sung before the nation views Him again: "This is the day which the LORD has made; let us rejoice and be glad in it. O LORD, do save, we beseech You; O LORD, we beseech You, do send prosperity! Blessed is the one who comes in the name of the Lord" (Ps. 118:24-26a).

How revealing it would have been to have witnessed Annas and Caiaphas as they audibly voiced the very Scripture references that God used to attest to His beloved Son. Did they glance at each other, as every line of the psalm pointed to some previous encounter with Jesus during the week leading up to His crucifixion, attempting to detect if the other caught the significance of what they both recited? Did the eyes of the one reflect the spiritual barrenness of the other? Perhaps each was lost in his own thoughts. More probably, fomenting disgust overrode all other emotions and reactions that would have resided in a more fertile heart, as the two leaders of Israel sang divinely inspired Messianic truths.

— The Stone and the Glory, pp. 130-31

DEEPER WALK STUDY

For those who want to research additional related Scripture and topics, consider the following:

Go back and reread "The Lesson" Parts 1 and 2 (in one sitting, if possible) and mark the Scripture passages in your Bible. Pay careful attention to the details of the Passover, and write out how God exercised sovereign control over all involved. One way to do this is to write a timeline of who is doing what at what time (that is, with the two different ways to begin the new day, write details about which group is doing what).

9

The Stumble

When most of us start studying the Bible, we do so by individual verses or certain portions of Scripture, which is not a bad place to begin. The deeper studies begin if you are able to go through entire books of the Bible. Even then what we are prone to do is to take the Bible and try to make it immediately applicable to our own world. It is much better to drop down into the world of the Bible and attempt "to see with their eyes and hear with their ears," and then make application section sense of "What can we learn about God from what we have learned?" or sometimes, "What biblical truths can we apply to our own lives?"

Simply put, it is our responsibility to drop down into the world of the Bible characters, particularly during the life of Jesus. This makes His already alive Word come alive even more. We have to know such things as what was the religious condition of the people at the time. Were they in obedience or disobedience to God? Also, what were the required religious feasts and sacrifices? For example, the Day of Atonement is often considered ancient and outdated information for most Christians (or many may be unaware that it even existed), yet the author of the Book of Hebrews expects his readers to understand the significance of this God-demanded (for the nation of Israel) national gathering. It is a lifetime study for all who do it, myself included. When we drop down into their world and hopefully do this right, it makes the already living and abiding Word of God (1 Pet. 1:22-23) become even "more alive" in our understanding.

This chapter shows the eternal striking contrast between the saved and the lost. In First Peter 2:6-8, we see that Peter employed three of the often quoted Stone prophecies, as well as the two different categories for those who believe or who disbelieve: "For this is contained in Scripture: 'Behold I lay in Zion a choice stone, a precious corner stone, and he who believes in Him shall not be disappointed.' This precious value, then, is for you who believe. But for those who disbelieve, 'The stone which the builders rejected, this became the very corner stone,' and, 'A stone of stumbling and a rock of offense'; for they stumble because they are disobedient to the word, and to this doom they were also appointed."

What a contrast Jude 24-25 presents for what God has promised for those who receive Him and walk with Him: "Now to Him who is able to keep you from stumbling, and to make you stand in the presence of His glory blameless with great joy, to the only God our Savior, through Jesus Christ our Lord, be glory, majesty, dominion and authority, before all time and now and forever. Amen."

SCRIPTURE REFERENCES

Key passages used in this chapter include: Leviticus 16, John 11:45-53, Luke 3:2, and Acts 5:17 and 23:8.

READING ASSIGNMENTS

Read chapter nine "The Stumble" before attempting to answer any of the following questions.

QUESTIONS FROM THE STONE AND THE GLORY

1. What is the significance of the Day of Atonement? What was unique about it? Explain (pp. 138-39).

    _____

    _____

    _____

    _____

2. What is the significance of the phrase "high priest that year"? What does this show about the priesthood, and why is this important? Explain (pp. 140-42).

    _____

    _____

    _____

    _____

3. What does the high priest and his family or associates have to do with the money that was kept in the Temple? How, then, would Jesus twice infuriate them? Explain (pp. 142-44).

    _____

    _____

    _____

    _____

4. What is the theological significance that for almost two centuries the High Priest of Israel was a Sadducee? Why was this horribly sad for the nation of Israel? Explain (pp. 143-45).

    _____

    _____

_____

_____

5. How does the change in the high priesthood demonstrate the disruption caused by the Gospel going forth? Why would the changes most likely occur? Explain (pp. 147-48).

_____

_____

_____

_____

6. How is it evident that Jesus' multiple use of Psalm 118 (especially in the life of Peter) bore "early fruit" in the Book of Acts (pp. 148-50)? Explain.

_____

_____

_____

_____

7. Why would the first Day of Atonement after Jesus was crucified be so different (pp. 150-52)? Explain.

_____

_____

_____

_____

8. Why does belief or unbelief in the Stone of Israel ultimately relate to everyone? Explain (pp. 154-55).

_____

_____

_____

_____

*B*ut Scripture gives more telling information about the beliefs of the Sadducees. Decades later in Acts 23, when Paul was on trial before the Sanhedrin, he appealed to his fellow Pharisees that he was on trial for the hope of the resurrection. A resulting vigorous argument erupted between the attending Pharisees and Sadducees. Luke added a most revealing verse that succinctly summarized the religion of the Sadducees: "For the Sadducees say that there is no resurrection, nor an angel, nor a spirit, but the Pharisees acknowledge them all" (Acts 23:8).

No resurrection. No angels. No spirit.

If the Sadducees were only a trade group or guild of varying relevance, they would have been a sect that would have rendered a great amount of damaging influence on the nation. But how much more—and how tragically sad for Israel—that for roughly the last two hundred years that the Temple had functioned, the high priest and his closest associates were all Sadducees. The High Priest of Israel—the one ordained by God's Word to enter the Holy of Holies once a year on the Day of Atonement—did not believe in the spiritual world. He and his associates would never accept Jesus' statement to the woman at the well, "God is spirit, and those who worship Him must worship in spirit and truth" (John 4:24). The truth to them was that the spiritual world did not exist. By claiming that angels do not exist, it logically follows that fallen angels and, ultimately, Satan are not real either. Not holding a belief in the resurrection would also require a lack of belief in either heaven or hell because, after all, the resurrected dead must have an abode in which to dwell.

—The Stone and the Glory, p. 144

QUESTIONS FROM THE WORD

1. What was unique about the high priest in both his clothing (on special occasions) and his function? Explain (pp. 135-39).

_____

_____

_____

_____

2. How did Jesus raising Lazarus from the dead add to the events of Passover week according to John 11:45-53? Why is this important? Explain (pp. 139-41).

_____

_____

_____

_____

3. Why is the phrase "in the high priesthood of Annas and Caiaphas" (Luke 3:2) so revealing (pp. 112-13)? What does this statement reveal about the high priesthood as it relates to John 11:49 and Acts 4:6? Explain (pp. 141-42).

_____

_____

_____

_____

4. Based on the information revealed in Acts 23:8, how would the Sadducees and the high priesthood's family approach John the Baptist? How do you know? How does this help explain John's exceedingly strong rebukes to them? Explain (pp. 143-45).

_____

_____

_____

_____

5. Scripture always presents the Sadducees in a negative manner. Compared with some of the other religious groups mentioned in the Gospels or Acts, why is this eternally important? Explain (pp. 150-52).

_____

_____

_____

_____

6. How does Paul use the two "Stone prophecies" in the Book of Romans? By reading the context of Romans 10, what was he proving by using these references, and why is this important? Explain (pp. 152-54).

_____

_____

_____

_____

7. From what you have read in the Bible and in *The Stone and the Glory*, why is it logical that Peter would quote Psalm 118:22 in his first epistle? Explain.

_____

_____

_____

_____

The advent of John the Baptist would have caused the Sadducees to approach in cunning curiosity. Surprisingly, some came to be baptized, but John would not permit it. Instead he rebuked them, saying, "You brood of vipers, who warned you to flee from the wrath to come? Therefore bear fruit in keeping with repentance; and do not suppose that you can say to yourselves, 'We have Abraham for our father'; for I say to you that from these stones God is able to raise up children to Abraham" (Matt. 3:7-9). For the Sadducees, coming to John was not an act of repentance; it was merely a reconnaissance. Also, John the Baptist knew them well enough to realize that their religious beliefs would not allow for any acceptance of him or his ministry. The Sadducees would never accept the story of the angel appearing to Zacharias—because, according to the Sadducees, angels do not exist. They would also reject the prophecies of Isaiah or Malachi, for these also were outside the Law of Moses. They especially would not accept John's pointing to Another, "As for me, I baptize you with water for repentance, but He who is coming after me is mightier than I, and I am not fit to remove His sandals; He will baptize you with the Holy Spirit and fire" (Matt. 3:11). Holy *Spirit?*—in a spiritual world that does not exist?

—The Stone and the Glory, pp. 144-45

THE HEART OF THE MATTER

Before moving on to the next section, you should be able to answer the following questions. If you are unable to answer the following questions biblically, study the appropriate sections again. (Remember: this section is intended only for review).

1. What was unique and important about the Day of Atonement (pp. 138-39)?

2. Why is the phrase "in the high priesthood of Annas and Caiaphas" (Luke 3:2) so revealing (pp. 141-42)?

3. What is the theological significance (and sadness) that for almost two centuries the High Priest of Israel was a Sadducee (pp. 142-44)?

4. How is it evident that Jesus' multiple uses of Psalm 118 (especially in the life of Peter) bore "early fruit" in the Book of Acts (pp. 148-50)?

5. What was so different about the first Day of Atonement after Jesus was crucified (pp. 150-52)?

6. How does Paul use the two "Stone prophecies" in the Book of Romans, and why is this important (pp. 152-54)?

7. Why does belief or unbelief in the Stone of Israel ultimately relate to everyone (pp. 154-55)?

PERSONAL APPLICATION SECTION

1. How does the terribly wicked high priesthood of Annas and Caiaphas contrast with the high priesthood of the ascended Jesus, especially as seen in Hebrews 7:23–8:2 (pp. 143-46)? What are some of these contrasts, and what can we give thanks to God about from this? Explain.

_____

_____

2. What are some of the events and truths from this chapter that you are thankful to God for? What are they, and why are they important? Explain these to someone else.

_____

_____

_____

_____

3. Write your own personal application question from this chapter (in other words, "what have I learned") that was not asked elsewhere and give the answer to your question.

_____

_____

_____

_____

*H*ow different was this first Day of Atonement after the resurrection of Messiah. How spiritually dead this stone-hearted one was who represented the people before a God that he did not know or believe existed.

Yet, with clock-like precision the high and holy day began. The high priest appeared before the people wearing the ornamentation of his "holy" office. After a few ritual confessions, he turned from the people to enter into the holy place of the Temple that eventually led into the holy of holies. Left alone with thoughts known only to him and God, he went about the prescribed procedure. While stoic about Levitical purity, other parts of this ritualistic routine must have seemed ridiculously absurd to one who would not accept the possibility of the resurrection. Why apply the blood for atonement when, after all, the absence or presence of atonement has no eternal consequence? Why have forgiveness of sins if there is no judgment in the afterlife? By what would the sins be removed? Even more important, by whom would they be removed? But the high priest continued, and by the jingling of his steps—caused by the God-ordained design of the hem of his garment—was heard by many outside who stood closest to the sanctuary.

Once inside and removed from the people's sight, the high priest was supposed to remove his high priestly attire. Would Annas? In virtually every respect he was at his heart a practicing atheist; a religious atheist, to be sure, but, nonetheless, one who denied the essentials of the faith. Why show reverence for a God that you are not sure exists? Perhaps, except for the prescribed bells and pomegranates attached to his hem, he would have skipped the designated undressing. But then again, perhaps not. After all, the Sadducees were known for their strict adherence to Levitical purity—outward purity anyway. Annas would be careful not to defile himself, such as when his associates would not enter the Roman Praetorium fearing they would defile themselves and be unable to celebrate the feast (John 18:28). The fact that they themselves were already putridly defiled would not enter into consciences that had long since ceased functioning as any safeguard.

— The Stone and the Glory, pp. 150-51

DEEPER WALK STUDY

For those who want to research additional related Scripture and topics, consider the following:

Read carefully and list the prescribed details in regarding the Day of Atonement in Leviticus 16-17.

Based on the information given in Acts 5:17 and 23:8 with either a concordance (if you have one) or by just going through your Bible, note every time that the high priest, chief priests, or Sadducees are mentioned in the Gospels and Acts. Write down how understanding their theology helps explain why John the Baptist first and Jesus later denounced and rebuked them.

10

The Two

I have the high privilege of studying for myself and also for teaching others the Word of God. And it is (for obvious reasons) in that order: studying and teaching. I enjoy both parts equally, but even if for some reason unknown to me that God would shut the door to teach or to preach, I would still want to study on my own. This is not so much as a professor; this is as a child of God (1 John 3:1-3). After all, the Greek root word for "disciple" means "learner," and any true child of God should continue to grow in "the grace and knowledge of our Lord Jesus Christ" (2 Pet. 3:18).

Samuel, Kings, and Chronicles is one of my favorite classes that I teach. The Hebrew Bible has these listed as three books; the English versions (which are man-made divisions) have them as six. There is nothing wrong with this; they both contain the same content.

Yet, often these books are grouped as part of the "historical books." Consequently, many well meaning Christians read them as one would read a history book. While it is true that that these books give descriptions of historical events, it is also true that they contain divine prophecies within them as well. Especially when you line up the prophets such as Habakkuk, Isaiah, Jeremiah, Ezekiel, and Daniel, God's prophetic light is even more revealing.

Many Christians are ignorant about these portions of Scripture thinking they have no future relevance in God's plan. It certainly seems from reading these portions that God has many prophecies to keep, and as we shall see in the upcoming chapters, they all somehow tie in with the person and work of "The Shepherd, the Stone of Israel" (Gen. 49:23). After all, the first verse of this chapter, Genesis 49:1, states, "Then Jacob summoned his sons and said, 'Assemble yourselves that I may tell you what will befall you in the days to come.'" How fitting that "days to come" is literally in the Hebrew "end of the days." So there very much is a prophetic element to this section.

Come soon Lord Jesus (Rev. 22:20)!

SCRIPTURE REFERENCES

So many key passages exist in this chapter. You may just want to highlight the references in your book or your Bible.

READING ASSIGNMENTS

Read chapter ten "The Two" before attempting to answer any of the following questions.

QUESTIONS FROM THE STONE AND THE GLORY

1. As repeatedly indicated in God's Word, if enemies attacked and defeated the Jewish people, what was the core problem and cause for this? Explain (pp. 159-60).

_____

_____

_____

_____

2. After Solomon's prayer in 1 Kings 8, what specific promises does God make in reference to His own Temple? What shows the everlasting aspect of His promise, even as it relates to the present time? Why is this promise so important? Explain (pp. 163-65).

_____

_____

_____

_____

3. How does the Book of Lamentations relate to the destruction of God's Temple? Explain (pp. 167-69).

_____

_____

_____

_____

4. What are the context, content, and significance of Daniel's prayer in Daniel 9? Why are these important as they relate to the future? Explain (pp. 169-71).

_____

_____

_____

_____

5. How much information did God put in His Word regarding the destruction of His Temple? Why would He do this? Explain (p. 171).

_____

6. What is the theological problem for any unsaved Bible-believing Jew (because many Jews exist who do not remotely believe that any of the Bible is true), as it relates to the second destruction of God's Temple in 70 AD? Explain what this is, and why this is important (pp. 171-73).

_____

_____

_____

_____

7. What is the great sin that the Jewish nation obviously committed or God *never* would have destroyed His Temple, as He has stated repeatedly in His Word? Why is this so important? Explain (pp. 173-74).

_____

_____

_____

_____

*A*s is true so many times in Scripture, God offers only two options: life or death, obedience or disobedience, the blessing or the curse, sheep or goats—heaven or hell. Such was and still is true for the Jewish people from that day forward, and many of the same truths apply to every person who has ever lived or who will ever live.

Each generation of the Jewish people knew exactly what awaited them—or at least should have known. When godly Joshua led the people to victory, it was because of the nation collectively being in covenant obedience that resulted in the covenant promise of victory that God had given (e.g. Deut. 28:7). When Joshua and his generation died (Joshua 1-2), the people quickly fell into spiritual sin, and just exactly as God had promised, *He* raised up multiple enemies in the times of the Judges. The Moabites and other invaders did not ravage the country by their own design; God raised them up to punish His disobedient people just as He had said He would. Read what is called the Old Testament and you will find His raising up of enemies occurring time and time again. In fact, the Mosaic Law became somewhat of a "spiritual barometer" for how the nation of Israel lived. If they were victorious in war, they were in covenant obedience to Yahweh; if they lost, the true problem did not indicate a lack of military capacity as much as it indicated that they were in covenant disobedience to Yahweh. The same is true for their crops, rain, drought—all were contingent on whether they lived in obedience to God or not.

—*The Stone and the Glory*, pp. 159-60

QUESTIONS FROM THE WORD

1. What is the importance of Leviticus 28 and Deuteronomy 28 as it relates to the blessing or the cursing of the nation of Israel? What does Leviticus 26:40-45 state in reference to future generations for Israel, and why is this important? Explain (pp. 157-60).

_____

_____

_____

_____

2. What are some of the particulars of Solomon's prayer in reference to God and His Temple? What does He ask God to do, and why? Why is this important? Explain (pp. 159-64).

_____

_____

_____

_____

3. How do Solomon's prayer (1 Kings 8:12-53) and God's reply (1 Kings 9:1-9) harmonize precisely with what God promised He would do based on Leviticus 26 and Deuteronomy 28? Show some examples (pp. 159-64).

_____

_____

_____

_____

4. What are some of the major themes of Jeremiah's two Temple messages (Jer. 7–10 and 26:1-6), especially in how they relate to God's Temple? Why is this important? Explain (pp. 165-69).

_____

_____

_____

_____

5. What is the importance of the summary statement of why God allowed His Temple to be destroyed (2 Chron. 36:15-21)? What does this indicate, and why is this important? Explain (pp. 169-70).

_____

_____

_____

_____

6. What is the importance of Jesus' teaching about Jerusalem and God's Temple as shown in Matthew 23:37-39 and 24:1-2? Explain (pp. 173-74).

_____

_____

_____

_____

Of special importance are the truths that go beyond Solomon's time. God promised in 1 Kings 9:3, "I have consecrated this house which you have built by putting My name there *forever*, and My eyes and My heart will be there *perpetually*." From the original day that God's Temple was dedicated onward, at all times His name in someway will be there, and His eyes will look upon His holy mountain. Technically speaking, as long as there is an earth, God's name and God's special look will always be there: even during the times of the Gentiles (Luke 21:24); even when Messiah was born, even when there is a pagan shrine on the site where the Holy of Holies was; these do not change anything: God has put His name there *forever*; God has placed His eyes there *perpetually*. However, Yahweh also promised that if the people were disobedient, He Himself would make His own house "a heap of ruins" so that everyone would be astounded. Ironically, all will know is that the Lord did this and why: because His people were not faithful to Him.

—*The Stone and the Glory*, p. 164

THE HEART OF THE MATTER

Before moving on to the next section, you should be able to answer the following questions. If you are unable to answer the following questions biblically, study the appropriate sections again. (Remember: this section is intended only for review).

1. As repeatedly indicated in God's Word, if enemies attacked and defeated the Jewish people, what was the core problem and cause for this (pp. 159-60)?

2. What does Leviticus 26:40-45 state in reference to future generations for Israel, and why is this important? Explain (pp. 157-60).

3. What shows the everlasting aspect of God's promise for His own Temple, and why is this promise so important (pp. 163-65)?

4. What is the importance of the summary statement (2 Chron. 36:15-21) of why God

allowed His Temple to be destroyed the first time (pp. 169-70)?

5. What are the context, content, and significance of Daniel's prayer in Daniel 9, and why are these important as they relate to the future (pp. 169-71)?

6. What is the theological problem for any unsaved Bible-believing Jew as it relates to the second destruction of God's Temple in AD 70? Why this is important (pp. 173-74)?

7. What is the great sin that the Jewish nation obviously committed or God *never* would have destroyed His Temple? Why is this so important (pp. 173-74)?

PERSONAL APPLICATION SECTION

1. What does King Solomon understand about the total depravity of all of mankind (1 Kings 8:46)? How would this verse later stand in contrast to how the Pharisees and other religious leaders (or even the rich young ruler) viewed themselves especially as seen in the Gospels? How can you use this teaching with anyone you meet (Jew or Gentile) who thinks that he or she has never sinned or who has kept all the commandments? Explain.

_____

_____

_____

_____

2. What have you learned about God the Father and Jesus in this chapter? Even though in many portions of the Scripture we have seen descriptions of terribly sad events, what can we thank God for in reference to His attributes and activities? Explain.

_____

_____

_____

_____

3. How can this chapter be useful in evangelizing currently unsaved Jewish people? Explain.

_____

_____

_____

_____

4. Write your own personal application question from this chapter (in other words,

"what have I learned") that was not asked elsewhere and give the answer to your question.

_____

_____

_____

_____

*A*ny Bible-believing Jew who at this point does not believe that the Messiah has already come, and thus currently has rejected Jesus, would readily acknowledge what is so evident in the Holy Word because it is repeated so many times: the only way possible that God's own Temple would or could ever be destroyed was if God Himself did it, and that being said, the only way that God would destroy His Temple was if the nation was living in blatant covenant disobedience before Him.

But that is exactly the problem. For an "Old Testament" believing Jew (not a Christian), an orthodox Jew, there is no good, logical explanation for the second destruction of God's Temple in 70 AD by the Romans on the exact same day of the year that God's first Temple was destroyed. With the first Temple, idolatry proliferated in the land (Ezek. 8); with the second Temple, there were no idols, no high places, no Baal worship. The Temple functioned; rabbis, Pharisees, Sadducees, priests; sacred days, fastidiously observed traditions, practices and sacrifices.

A currently unsaved Torah-believing Jew can explain the fall of the first Temple as easily as Daniel could in the prayer of Daniel 9. God gave a great number of warnings from His Word of what was to come as prophet after prophet bore witness.

— *The Stone and the Glory*, pp. 172-73

DEEPER WALK STUDY

For those who want to research additional related Scripture and topics, consider the following:

Carefully read through the many Bible references listed in this chapter and the contexts with them, if you like. Make a list of the multiple references to God's Temple noting especially what He promised to do in the past and in the future.

Also, place them beside the single pronouncement of Jesus in Matthew 23:37-39 and 24:1-2. Notice the vast different in the amount of content given in God's Word, but note especially that they both came true, and how Jesus stands alone in His predictions.

11

The Return

"The Return" chapter of this book is very similar in format to "The Exchange" chapter in *The Darkness and the Glory*. I did not purposely set out to make them similar; I just noticed this after it had been written. In "The Exchange" there are multiple exchanges that take place almost like concentric circles that expand when a rock is thrown into a lake or pond. The same occurs in this chapter, as multiple returns exist—all ultimately related to the life and work of the Messiah.

This was a very enjoyable chapter to research and to write. After all, we are getting closer to the Glory.

SCRIPTURE REFERENCES

There are too many key Scripture passages in this chapter to list. I suggest that you mark them either in your Bible or in your book or in both.

READING ASSIGNMENTS

Read chapter eleven "The Return" before attempting to answer any of the following questions.

QUESTIONS FROM THE STONE AND THE GLORY

1. From what we have studied so far, why is the account of the shepherds in Luke 2 so important as it relates to the glory of God? Why is this important? Explain (pp. 175-78).

_____

_____

_____

_____

2. Did the glory of God return to earth the night Jesus was born? Why or why not, and why is this important? Explain (p. 178).

    _____

    _____

    _____

    _____

3. Summarize the visit of the shepherds to Joseph, Mary and Jesus. How did Joseph and Mary know that the shepherds' account was accurate? Explain (pp. 180-82).

    _____

    _____

    _____

    _____

4. What are the significant factors of Mary's taking the baby Jesus to the Temple for the first time? Explain (pp. 182-83).

    _____

    _____

    _____

    _____

5. Who was Simeon? Why would Joseph and Mary be amazed at what he said (Luke 2:33)? How does God show that He was the One who orchestrated this divine appointment? Explain and show examples (pp. 183-85).

    _____

    _____

    _____

    _____

6. How is the glory of God connected with the second coming of Jesus? Why is this important? Explain (pp. 187-90).

    _____

    _____

    _____

    _____

*I*n a way quite similar to the Tabernacle and the Temple containing God's glory centuries before, so it was with His Son: in a way, yet infinitely distinct, God's glory inhabited the Son. Sometime nearly thirty years after His birth, Jesus merely showed what was His in essence and by nature at the Transfiguration (Matt. 17:1-9; Mark 9:2-8; Luke 9:29-36). To enter earth's domain, Jesus had willingly laid aside equality with God and had taken on the form of a bondservant (Phil. 2:5-11). If the Trinity had so determined, Jesus could have revealed the glory that was His anytime He wanted, to whom He wanted, and in the degree He wanted—even when being spat upon, scourged, and crucified. For the most part, Jesus chose not to reveal His glory, leaving that display instead to His pending return to earth, as dozens of prophecies bear divine promise.

So on the night that Jesus was born, it would not be fitting to have the glory of God reside in the heavens when the Glory of God had been born on earth. And in a real sense, the body of Jesus was the Temple that the glory of God inhabited. Jesus was the means by which God would dwell (or "tabernacle") among His people (John 1:14). God's majestic glory, greater than all His creations, became temporarily encased in the body of Jesus. That God's glory would inhabit a place so small should not be surprising. Even the Ark of the Covenant built during the Exodus generation is about the size of a coffin. It must have caused the devout in Israel to ponder: *You mean the glory of God can take up residence in something about the size of a human body?*

Of course. God did so with the Ark. He did so in Jesus.

—*The Stone and the Glory*, pp. 179-80

QUESTIONS FROM THE WORD

1. What is the importance of John 2:13-21 and Matthew 26:57-61 as it relates to the glory of God and His Temple, or does it? Explain (pp. 178-80).

_____

_____

_____

_____

2. Summarize the visit of the shepherds to Joseph, Mary, and the baby Jesus. How did Joseph and Mary know that what the shepherds said had happened to them was true? Explain (pp. 180-82).

_____

_____

_____

_____

3. What is the importance of Galatians 4:4? How does this relate to Luke 2:21-22 and Leviticus 12:1-7? What does this tell us about the parents of Jesus?

Explain (pp. 181-83).

_____

_____

_____

_____

4. How does Revelation 13:5-8 and 2 Thessalonians 2:4 reveal that God will divinely authorize horrible blasphemy for a limited time during the Tribulation? Why is this important? Explain (pp. 186-87).

_____

_____

_____

_____

5. What are the important factors of Ezekiel's prophecies as they relate to the glory of God? Why are these important? Explain (pp. 189-93).

_____

_____

_____

_____

So when Simeon declared that he had witnessed God's salvation, "a light of revelation to the Gentiles, and the glory of Your people Israel," this was not new revelation—this was new affirmation. Not that Mary and Joseph needed personal assurance, but it no doubt crossed their minds as to how many others also knew the true identity of their Child.

Their amazement was not about the content of Simeon's statement as much as it was about how this stranger had access to these truths. If Mary and Joseph said anything, it would not have been, "What do you mean?" Instead, it would be more along the lines of, "How do you know this" or "Who told you these things?"

Why, God did, of course.

In the midst of a high priesthood that did not believe in the spiritual world, God sent one as a prophetic witness in the midst of spiritual darkness. It is not a random occurrence that in three successive verses Luke penned a reference to the Holy Spirit of God. Simeon was a man whom "the Holy Spirit was upon Him" (Luke 2:25). "And it had been revealed to him by the Holy Spirit that he would not see death before he had seen the Lord's Christ" (Luke 2:26). For one who walked so closely with God, it should not be surprising that his rendezvous would likewise come from God's leading: "And he came in the Spirit into the Temple" (Luke 2:27). And so Simeon, by the Spirit, identified the same One whom John the Baptist had identified even while in his mother's womb.

What Simeon disclosed was actually more than what the shepherds had understood. They were told about the birth—and went to see—the promised Messiah. Simeon knew that more was needed: God's Salvation; God's Light; God's Savior—God's Glory. Appropriately, though, Simeon identified that the Light and the Glory had returned—briefly—to the Temple of God where God's special presence had not resided for over six hundred years.

—The Stone and the Glory, p. 185

THE HEART OF THE MATTER

Before moving on to the next section, you should be able to answer the following questions. If you are unable to answer the following questions biblically, study the appropriate sections again. (Remember: this section is intended only for review).

1. From what we have studied so far, why is the account of the shepherds in Luke 2 so important as it relates to the glory of God (pp. 175-78)?

2. What are the significant factors of Mary's taking the baby Jesus to the Temple for the first time? Explain (pp. 182-83).

3. How does God show that He was the One who orchestrated the divine appointment with Simeon and Joseph, and Mary, and Jesus (pp. 183-85)?

4. How does Revelation 13:5-8 and 2 Thessalonians 2:4 reveal that God will divinely authorize horrible blasphemy for a limited time during the Tribulation, and why is this important (pp. 186-87)?

5. How is the glory of God connected with the second coming of Jesus, and why is this important (pp. 187-90)?

6. What are the important factors of Ezekiel's prophecies as they relate to the glory of God, and why are these important (pp. 189-93)?

PERSONAL APPLICATION SECTION

1. In this chapter, what are some of the examples of grace that make you appreciate the Trinity more? Name some and thank God.

_____

_____

_____

_____

2. How unique the testimonies of both Joseph and Mary will for us to hear when we get to heaven. How did God lovingly disciple this chosen couple before the birth of Jesus and almost immediately thereafter? Even though our stories are different, are there

ways in which God has lovingly discipled you in a growing understanding of who He is and how much He loves you? Name some examples, and tell this to others.

_____

_____

_____

_____

3. What have you learned about Jesus in this chapter that you want to tell someone else? Who is it and why?

_____

_____

_____

_____

4. Based on what you have read in this chapter, how is your life to be lived differently? Why?

_____

_____

_____

_____

5. Write your own personal application question from this chapter (in other words, "what have I learned") that was not asked elsewhere and give the answer to your question.

_____

_____

_____

_____

*I*n spite of his unequaled power and dominion, the Antichrist's rule will be lacking the glory of God. For blind inhabitants of the earth who will "not receive the love of the truth so as to be saved" (2 Thess. 2:10) and who will "not believe the truth, but took pleasure in wickedness" (2 Thess. 2:12), nothing else dazzles them as much as Satan's power and glory. The Antichrist will have only the glory of the nations (Luke 4:5-6). For people who have no true standard of assessment, the glory of the fallen world often substitutes for the glory of God. Paul revealed in 2 Corinthians 4:3-4, "And even if our gospel is veiled, it is veiled to those who are perishing, in whose case the god of this world has blinded the minds of the unbelieving so that they might not see the light of the gospel of the glory of Christ, who is the image of God." During the Tribulation, this blinding will be on a much more intensive scale.

At the return of Jesus, the world will recognize the difference between the glory of God and anything else; however, for the vast majority, it will be an understanding only as they receive the divine judgment. We should also note another important truth: the Antichrist will be able to seat himself in the rebuilt Temple during the Tribulation, much as the pagans before him entered into the abandoned Holy of Holies. God's glory does not return until Jesus returns (Matt. 16:27); therefore, the Temple of the Tribulation will not have God's glory. Whereas Nebuchadnezzar of Babylon's troops could not enter the holy of holies until God had removed His glory, so the Antichrist will be able to enter only because of the absence of God's glory—and by God's sovereign decree.

— The Stone and the Glory, pp. 188-89

DEEPER WALK STUDY

For those who want to research additional related Scripture and topics, consider the following:

Trace through and write out the Scripture references within this chapter and write out a summary of what these verses teach.

12

The Glory

*I*always enjoy whenever it is time to write "The Glory" chapter in any of the glory books. To me it is though we get to walk up this long and sometimes arduous mountain in order to gain a view that we would not otherwise be able to see. As many who go to the top of a mountain can testify, "the view from the top is well worth the effort."

I never want to hurry through "The Glory" chapters, but every time it ends the same way: these are only small samplings out of God's Word about His glory. My response after savoring the view is, "Let's go down and walk up another one and see the view from there!" I will have to see how God leads in this. I am still trying not to run ahead of Him, a lifetime lesson for me.

Yet, as much as I enjoy "The Glory" chapters, I must go back to the "His Cup—The Beginning" and the following first four chapters of *The Darkness and the Glory*. None of the truths that we have read in *The Stone and the Glory* would have been true unless He completely drank the entirety of "the cup which the Father had given Him" (John 18:11). While I long to go home and be with the Lord, "The Separation" chapter reminds me of the eternal state of the lost. That fact should not be lost from our walk and ministry as well.

So, let us dwell on His glory, but let us also be about the Lord's work until He returns for us either individually or collectively.

Come soon, Lord Jesus!

SCRIPTURE REFERENCES

Key passages used in this chapter include Exodus 32–34, 1 Corinthians, and 2 Corinthians 1–5.

READING ASSIGNMENTS

Read chapter twelve "The Glory" before attempting to answer any of the following questions.

QUESTIONS FROM THE STONE AND THE GLORY

1. What effect did being in the very presence of God have on Moses? How did the

nation of Israel respond to this and why? Explain (pp. 199-200).

_____

_____

_____

_____

2. How does Second Corinthians relate to Exodus 32–34? Name some important matters from this (pp. 202-205).

_____

_____

_____

_____

3. How does the Transfiguration of Jesus relate to the glory of God and the return of Jesus to earth? How does this relate to Moses? Explain (pp. 205-207).

_____

_____

_____

_____

4. How does Paul use the account of Moses and the glory of God on Moses' face to contrast the blessings God has given for those who are New Covenant participants? What is Paul's logic, and why is this important? Explain (pp. 208-210).

_____

_____

_____

_____

5. Summarize the similarities and contrasts between the glory of God on the face of Moses and what we who are saved have in Christ (pp. 211-213). Why are these important? Explain.

_____

_____

_____

_____

God removed His visual presence from the people, and yet He would speak to Moses face to face. Fortunately, God allows us a peak at what the two friends spoke. For Moses, there was still that major problem that needed God's immediate attention: "Then Moses said to the LORD, 'See, You say to me, "Bring up this people!" But You Yourself have not let me know whom You will send with me'" (Exod. 32:12). God had promised to send His angel, but not Himself—and this greatly concerned Moses. The following conversation expresses Moses' anguish as a leader as well as his heart's desire as an individual:

And He [God] said, "My presence shall go with you, and I will give you rest."

Then he [Moses] said, "If Your presence does not go with us, do not lead us up from here. For how then can it be known that I have found favor in Your sight, I and Your people? Is it not by Your going with us, so that we, I and Your people, may be distinguished from all the other people who are upon the face of the earth?"

The presence of God dwelling in the very midst of the people was not just some spiritual novelty. As far as Moses was concerned, it was mandatory; essential; life-giving. Moses and the nation were there that day only because of the presence and covenant faithfulness of Yahweh. Although neither the tabernacle nor the Temple had yet been built, if God removed His presence from their midst, they may as well not go any farther—especially since they would soon perish from either the physical elements or from their enemies.

—The Stone and the Glory, pp. 197-98

QUESTIONS FROM THE WORD

1. What is Israel's blatant sin in Exodus 32? How did God respond in Exodus 33? Why did this greatly trouble Moses? Explain (pp. 195-98).

_____

_____

_____

_____

2. What were some of the major problems in the Corinthian church that Paul was forced to address? How does this set the stage for the writing of Second Corinthians? Explain (pp. 200-203).

_____

_____

_____

_____

3. How does 1 Corinthians 10:1-4 help explain matters related to Exodus 33-34 (pp. 205-207)? Explain.

_____

_____

_____

_____

4. How does 2 Corinthians 6 relate to Exodus 29:43-45 and Leviticus 26:11-12? Why is this important? Explain (pp. 210-11).

_____

_____

_____

_____

*B*ut still—something is not right. It does not seem to fit that in some ways the analogy that Paul—and the Holy Spirit—employed has more contrasts than similarities. We would think there should be more relevance than this. You certainly would not read Exodus 32–34 and conclude that this is obviously true for the Apostle Paul. After all, if I were a Corinthian critic of Paul and if I had received this chapter, I would question him, "If your gospel is so glorious, why do not people stampede to it?" Paul would answer: "And even if our gospel is veiled, it is veiled to those who are perishing, in whose case the god of this world has blinded the minds of the unbelieving so that they might not see the light of the gospel of the glory of Christ, who is the image of God" (2 Cor. 4:3-4).

How appropriate that Satan blinds the minds of unbelievers, specifically so that they might not see the light of the gospel of Christ's glory. Trinkets of materialism, pride, sex, worldly fame—whatever works. Blind them to the glory of God—keep them in veiled bondage, ignorant of both the glory and the solution. That is all Satan has to do to keep one from a saving relationship with Jesus. Broad, indeed, is the way to destruction (Matt. 7:13).

—*The Stone and the Glory*, pp. 204-205

THE HEART OF THE MATTER

Before moving on to the next section, you should be able to answer the following questions. If you are unable to answer the following questions biblically, study the appropriate sections again. (Remember: this section is intended only for review).

1. What effect did being in the very presence of God have on Moses? How did the nation of Israel respond to this and why (pp. 199-200)?

2. How does Second Corinthians relate to Exodus 32–34 (pp. 202-205)?

3. How does the Transfiguration of Jesus relate to the glory of God and the return of Jesus to earth? How does this relate to Moses (pp. 205-207)?

4. How does Paul use the account of Moses and the glory of God on his face to contrast the blessings God has given for those who are New Covenant participants (pp. 208-210)?

5. How does 2 Corinthians 6 relate to Exodus 29:43-45 and Leviticus 26:11-12, and why is this important (pp. 210-11)?

6. Summarize the similarities and contrasts between the glory of God on the face of Moses and what we who are saved have in Christ (pp. 211-13).

PERSONAL APPLICATION SECTION

1. What have you learned in this chapter that makes you appreciate the power of Jesus? Explain.

_____

_____

_____

_____

2. What have you learned in this chapter that makes you appreciate the grace of Jesus? Explain to someone else.

_____

_____

_____

_____

3. Based on what you have read in this chapter, how is your life to be lived differently? Why?

_____

_____

_____

_____

4. Write your own personal application question from this chapter (in other words, "what have I learned") that was not asked elsewhere and give the answer to your question.

_____

_____

_____

_____

*A*lthough we have left out more than we have put in about this account, we have set the table for what we need for our present study. We need to make the appropriate connections in Scripture. One item to note is that the word "transfigure" is from the Greek verb from which we get our English word *metamorphosis*. Another very important consideration is that the word "transfigure"—this same word used to describe the Transfiguration of Jesus—occurs in only two other places in Scripture. One is in the famous verses of Romans 12:1-2: "Therefore I urge you, brethren, by the mercies of God, to present your bodies a living and holy sacrifice, acceptable to God, which is your spiritual service of worship. And do not be conformed to this world, but be *transformed* by the renewing of your mind, so that you may prove what the will of God is, that which is good and acceptable and perfect."

The same type of transforming (or transfigured, the same Greek word for the Gospel accounts) that Jesus had, we are to have in our lives. Notice the usage is passive, "be transformed"—not the active "transform yourselves." We draw near to God. We become spiritual sacrifices. We are not to be conformed to the world's standard and procedures—and then God will do the transforming, as our minds are renewed, especially by feeding on God's Word and by being in communal fellowship with Him.

Paul wrote a command in Romans 12:2 that believers are to be transformed by the renewing of their minds. He also wrote the only other remaining use of this word in the New Testament. But this time he wrote a statement, not an instruction. By this other usage of the word "transform" he uncovered a startling spiritual truth. Other than in the Transfiguration accounts in the Gospel and the one reference in Romans 12:2, the only other time this word for transfigure or transform occurs is back in the section of Second Corinthians where Paul used Moses as a contrasting example for the glory of the New Covenant—and a definitive statement of where God's glory currently dwells.

—*The Stone and the Glory*, pp. 207-208

DEEPER WALK STUDY

For those who want to research additional related Scripture and topics, consider the following:

Trace through and write out the Scripture references within this chapter and write out a summary of what these verses teach.

Reread the book.

Study Guide Summary Questions

1. What are your favorite (or most significant in your life) four or five things that you have learned from this study? List them and explain why they affected you so.

_____

_____

_____

_____

_____

_____

_____

2. How is your understanding of God different? Explain and give three or four examples.

_____

_____

_____

_____

_____

_____

_____

3. How is your understanding of yourself different? Explain and give examples.

_____

_____

_____

_____

_____

_____

_____

4. With whom do you look forward to sharing what you have learned in this study? Why?

_____

_____

_____

_____

_____

_____

_____

5. From what you have learned in your study, write out what you are thankful to God for that either He has already done in your life or else what is promised in His Word.

_____

_____

_____

_____

_____

_____

_____

6. By the way, as a reminder from a previous study, so what do you pray for . . . when you pray?

_____

_____

_____

_____

_____

_____

_____

_____